Understanding
and
Engaging
Adolescents

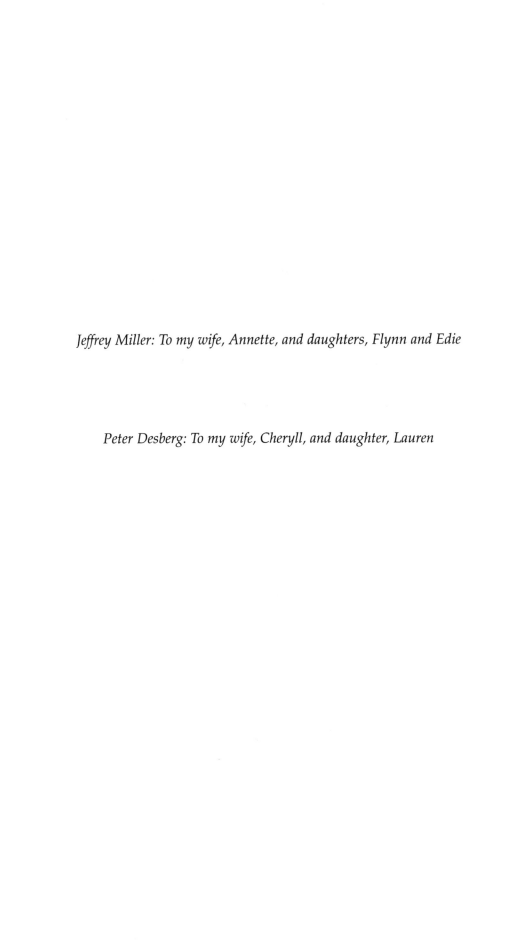

Jeffrey Miller: To my wife, Annette, and daughters, Flynn and Edie

Peter Desberg: To my wife, Cheryll, and daughter, Lauren

Understanding
and
Engaging
Adolescents

Jeffrey Miller   Peter Desberg

CORWIN
A SAGE Company

For information:

Corwin
A SAGE Company
2455 Teller Road
Thousand Oaks, California 91320
(800) 233-9936
Fax: (800) 417-2466
www.corwinpress.com

SAGE Ltd.
1 Oliver's Yard
55 City Road
London EC1Y 1SP
United Kingdom

SAGE Pvt. Ltd.
B 1/I 1 Mohan Cooperative
    Industrial Area
Mathura Road, New Delhi 110 044
India

SAGE Asia-Pacific Pte. Ltd.
33 Pekin Street #02-01
Far East Square
Singapore 048763

Printed in the United States of America

Library of Congress Cataloging-in-Publication Data

Miller, Jeffrey, 1966-
Understanding and engaging adolescents/Jeffrey Miller and Peter Desberg.
      p. cm.
Includes bibliographical references and index.
ISBN 978-1-4129-7000-6 (cloth)
ISBN 978-1-4129-7001-3 (pbk.)
   1. Middle school teaching. 2. High school teaching. 3. Teacher-student relationships.
4. Motivation in education. 5. Classroom management. I. Desberg, Peter. II. Title.

LB1623.M56 2009
373.1102—dc22   2009003336

This book is printed on acid-free paper.

09   10   11   12   13   10   9   8   7   6   5   4   3   2   1

Acquisitions Editor:	Jessica Allan
Editorial Assistant:	Joanna Coelho
Production Editor:	Veronica Stapleton
Copy Editor:	Tina Hardy
Typesetter:	C&M Digitals (P) Ltd.
Proofreader:	Sue Irwin
Cover Designer:	Karine Hovsepian

Contents

Preface

Several years ago, I submitted a proposal to speak at the California League of Middle Schools (CLMS) conference in San Diego. I had a Friday midafternoon slot from 2:35–3:35 p.m. The title of my presentation was "Motivating the Academically Unmotivated Student." Unfortunately, I woke up that morning feeling under the weather. I was sick enough that the thought of driving five hours to deliver a one-hour presentation wasn't motivation enough for me to get out of bed and drive from Los Angeles to San Diego. My talk was scheduled in a room that would accommodate between 25–30 people and the time slot was usually a poorly attended one. I called the conference organizers to cancel, chugged down some cold medicine, bundled up, and closed my eyes. At 2:32 p.m., I was awakened by the phone and heard a frantic voice on the other end. The woman identified herself as a CLMS representative and asked if I could get to the conference immediately. I told her that I was sick, in bed, in Los Angeles. I was thinking, "Didn't she get my message? What's the big deal? People cancel all the time." She said the interest in my presentation was a bit bigger than expected. She wanted to know if I could get there early in the morning and present the next day. She said, "There are well over 200 people wanting to hear your talk." Those words echoed in my head for a few minutes. Since I had the talk already prepared, I told her I would wake up early and drive to San Diego.

I arrived in San Diego around 7:40 a.m. and walked to the conference registration desk. There were signs everywhere: "Motivating the Academically Unmotivated with Dr. Jeff Miller moved to the Grand Ballroom at 8:00 a.m." Within educational circles, this was as close to rock stardom as I had ever been. I walked to the registration table. When I told them my name, there was a lot of hustling about and they escorted me to the Grand Ballroom. When I got there, about 50 people were already waiting. By 7:59 a.m., the room was packed. My PowerPoint presentation was being projected on a huge screen. At 8:00 a.m., I cleared my throat and just looked out at the audience members. They were eagerly awaiting what they hoped would be the magic remedy for motivating middle school students. I opened my mouth and the following words inadvertently popped out: "This is pathetic! How can this be the hottest topic at a state conference? Are you telling me that middle school students are that tough to motivate?"

Every head in the room nodded as one. That was the moment I knew this book *had* to be written. Our job as middle school teachers is the most daunting in K–12 education. The talk went well and I stayed around for over an hour talking to people. I was surprised to see how much the needs of middle school teachers are frighteningly similar to the students they teach. They needed to be listened to. Everyone has a story. As you read through this book, know that it is a series of activities mixed with a basic understanding of motivation and learning so the strategies have a better chance to stick with you.

The activities and strategies that we present in this book have a few things in common. They have all been battle-tested and *they work*. They are based on the best understanding from the fields of cognitive science, educational psychology, developmental psychology, social psychology, and pedagogical theory. We hope that we have actually written an "untextbook." We wrote this book with the intention of it being user-friendly, valuable, and as jargon-free as possible. At a party, a man was asked what he did for a living. He answered, "I'm an editor for an educational book company. It's my job to edit out the interesting parts." He did not work on this book.

Note that one of the conventions we have used throughout this text is writing in first person. We do this because we both like to tell stories. There is a great deal of research today which shows that stories teach better than preachy-type lecture or academic-dry writing. In case you are curious as to which one of us is telling which story, use this simple test. I am five feet ten inches tall and Jeff is six feet six inches tall. It the story feels tall, it's Jeff. I tell short stories. We hope you enjoy what we have to say.

Acknowledgments

Corwin gratefully acknowledges the following peer reviewers for their editorial insight and guidance:

David Callaway
8th-Grade Language Arts Teacher
Rocky Heights Middle School
Highlands Ranch, CO

Gustava Cooper-Baker
Principal
George Washington Carver Elementary School
Kansas City, MO

Jolene Dockstader
7th-Grade Language Arts Teacher
Jerome Middle School
Jerome, ID

Dolores Hennessy
Reading Specialist
Sarah Noble Intermediate School
New Milford, CT

Holly Johnson
Middle School Language Arts Teacher
University of Cincinnati
Cincinnati, OH

Kathryn McCormick
7th-Grade Teacher NBCT
Gahanna Middle School East
Gahanna, OH

Darcia Narvaez
Associate Professor
Department of Psychology
University of Notre Dame
Notre Dame, IN

About the Authors

 **Jeffrey Miller** completed his PhD in 2001 with a focus on motivation and learning in adolescent classrooms. He spent eight years teaching middle school in urban Los Angeles and four years designing student success programs at Santa Monica College. Currently, he teaches courses in educational psychology and classroom management at California State University, Dominguez Hills. Dr. Miller is the managing director of the Miller Consulting Group and provides consultation and professional development to schools within Los Angeles and across the country where he delivers keynote addresses and facilitates schools through organizational change.

 **Peter Desberg** is a professor of graduate education and coordinator of the Technology Based Education MA Program at California State University, Dominguez Hills. He is also a licensed clinical psychologist. Dr. Desberg is the author of 20 books and is a frequent presenter and keynote speaker at national conventions. He was the host of Introduction to Computers on the Los Angeles Unified School District's cable channel for 10 years and has appeared on many television shows. He also has been written about in many newspapers and magazines, including *Psychology Today, The Wall Street Journal, Cosmopolitan,* and *Reader's Digest.*

Part 1

The Theory

1 In the Beginning

Enthusiasm No Substitute for Wisdom

In 1992, public schools were being restructured and the sixth grade was getting ready to transition to middle school. I was getting my teaching credential that summer, and I was eager to find my first teaching job. I had recently found my passion for educating others while teaching English in Japan, and I found that I liked novelty and I even liked the challenge of dealing with a little discomfort. I wanted a real challenge. My goal was to teach in the toughest environment possible. I was looking for a teaching job in Los Angeles, a city that was rebuilding itself after the unrest following the Rodney King verdict. Finding a challenging school environment in Los Angeles was easy. I accepted a job at a "Ten Schools Program" school. The name identified it as one of the 10 lowest performing elementary schools in the Los Angeles Unified School District. My new sixth-grade class would really need a caring, dedicated, talented teacher to help move students through the school year, and I was sure I was that teacher.

I was hired on a Thursday and told to start the following Monday. I spent the entire weekend getting my room ready. I placed the desks into pods. I created lively bulletin boards and wrote out a nameplate for each student. I put up a huge tie-dyed sheet on the wall for colorful decoration. I brought in my old stereo so we could have music in our classroom. I wasn't just ready; I was "pumped."

I met my new students on the yard and walked them back to class. I asked them to find their nameplates so they could find their seats and sit down quietly. I had rehearsed my opening monologue in my head countless times. Now, it was show time. "Class," I began, "My name is Jeff. I understand you've already had three substitute teachers so far this school year. I am excited to be your teacher and want you to know that I care about you and your education. I plan on proving this all year long *by staying.*" There—I put it all out to them. What I didn't realize at that moment was that I had introduced myself by saying *nothing.* I swaggered in with soaring self-confidence and obvious commitment to helping these kids. I assumed that they would sense this and immediately believe it. I did nothing to *demonstrate* any of it.

My class proved this to me by getting out of control very quickly. By my third week, there was a chair fight, a full-on brawl, right in the middle of my classroom. Not knowing what else to do, I went over to a table and kicked it out of frustration—*hard.* Since I am a big, athletic guy, I kicked it hard enough to shatter the table. The kids froze, then jumped back into their seats and remained motionless. I finally had their attention. In the silence, I pointed at the table and yelled, "The next one of you that breathes without my permission will end up like *that.*" Through the haze in my head, I knew there had to be a better way to handle the situation.

I made many critical mistakes in this short time period. The most fundamental mistake I made was that I expected the students to like me. I expected them to *want* to work for me simply because I told them I cared about them. It's no accident that there are so many generations that have heard the phrase, "Actions speak louder than words." I didn't *show* the kids that I cared about them; I *told* them. However, the bigger mistake was that I wasn't appropriately prepared. Although I planned out my first few words, I didn't plan beyond that. I thought it wouldn't be necessary because by then, they would all like me. I failed to map out the first 15 minutes of my introduction. I winged it, and that is a mistake I never made again. Later, we discuss the importance of the first 15 minutes of the semester or year. However, before talking about change, it's important to see why there is so much reluctance to change.

To Change or Not to Change

Why do teachers resist change? Teachers are often in a position where change is mandated. There is an old joke: "How many psychologists does it take to change a light bulb?" The answer is this: "One, but the light bulb really has to want to change." While the joke may not be so funny, the point it makes is significant.

It's hard for people to change even when they really do want to change. When told they must, it's way more difficult. Teachers are often in this situation. They must change every time their state credential committee enacts new standards. They are also accountable to principals, department chairs, and parents.

In addition to being forced to change, the entire process of change is stressful. First, it often forces teachers out of their comfort zones. If you have watched an older teacher who is unfamiliar and uncomfortable with new technology, you know how much resistance you get in moving some teachers out of their comfort zones (Mach, et. al., 2005). When they are told that they must now infuse it, you often see incredibly creative forms of resistance. They are used to closing the door of their classroom and facing their students as the *expert*. They don't want to be thrust into a situation where their middle school students know way more than they do.

In many cases, change means having to learn. I often see university faculty using outdated textbooks because they don't want to go through the effort of having to read a new one and learn a lot of new information. Many teachers don't think the effort necessary for all that head-throbbing learning is worth the rewards they will get from it.

Teachers don't like uncertainty. It's stressful. They like to know what to expect from any action they take. Change eliminates predictability and replaces it with uncertainty. If you walk in the first day of class and present your rules, you know what to expect. If you change and have your students decide what the rules should be, it could work very smoothly, or it could lead to arguments and chaos. It's too big a risk for many teachers.

Wisdom, Not Experience

After I got some experience as a middle school teacher, I learned a lot about how to motivate my kids. One of the things I did was come in an hour before school started and stay an hour after so that I would be available for students who needed my help or just wanted to talk with me. That was one of the ways I learned to show them I cared about them. Many of my students came in just to hang out instead of talking to me about their problems. It was a very effective bonding procedure.

Whenever I run inservice workshops for middle school teachers, I make the suggestion that they try this approach. The first few times I mentioned it, I was surprised to hear the amount of hostility I got from many of them. My first reaction to them was an antagonistic one. Why weren't they more dedicated to their jobs? After talking to many middle school teachers, I changed my view drastically. Just about every one of them went into teaching with the dream of helping kids. Just as a rock will erode after years of water dripping on it, middle school teachers' fantasies erode as unmotivated, discourteous, antagonistic, uninterested middle school students keep dripping on them. I went in looking for an extra hour a day and found *the death of hope*.

To protect themselves, many teachers have learned to withdraw, become guarded, develop armor and fight apathy with apathy. In way too many cases, we see veteran teachers *burned out* and *hanging on* until they can retire. It is our goal to end this vicious cycle and restore the hopes and dreams you had when you first became a teacher, unless you got into it for the money, in which case you're well beyond our help. In this section, we examine the topic of *impression management*.

Impression Management

Impression management looks at two things: (1) how you are judged by others and (2) what factors you can control to help shape those judgments. In his book, *Blink: The Power of Thinking Without Thinking*, Malcolm Gladwell (2005) writes about a fascinating bit of research on teacher evaluation. College students viewed a 10-second video segment, and based on that short sample, evaluated how much they liked that college professor. Then they took a course from that very teacher and evaluated him again at the end of the course. The two evaluations, 10 seconds before taking the course and at the end of an entire course, showed a correlation of 80%. If that seems amazing, I have omitted a huge fact that makes this study even more amazing. The researchers stripped off the sound on the 10-second video. The students only *saw* the instructor teaching. They didn't even get to *hear* him. *Students make their judgments about you very quickly and accurately.*

When you walk into the room on that first day of school and utter your first few words, your students have pretty much made their decisions about you, and how you will all get along. You literally have a honeymoon period of a few minutes to create the impression that will help or haunt you for a semester or an entire year (Leary, 1996). *What* you say, *how* you say it, and most important, *how you back it up*, will create that impression. So, how and where should you start?

The Three Cs for Presenting Yourself to Your Class

Fortunately for you, educational psychologists have researched this question quite a bit, and surprisingly, most agree on where to start. You start with the three Cs: *caring, credibility,* and *competence*. They have a very interesting relationship to each other.

Caring

Telling students that you care about them is easy, fast, and vastly inadequate by itself. Caring helps only if your students believe that you really *do* care about them. This vital fact brings the idea of credibility into play.

Credibility

You can tell students anything you want, but for them to believe it, you have to *do* things that make what you told them credible. In the section that follows, we suggest several things you can do to help get students to believe both that you care and that you are competent. I have seen teachers tell kids that they will always be supportive, no matter what. Then, unfortunately, a student does something that really does require an advocate, and the teacher is not there for that student. Credibility has to be *proven repeatedly*, but it can be destroyed with *one* bad act.

Competence

You have to let students know that you are *capable* of delivering what you claim. Once again, you have to tell them why you are competent and then back it up to make it credible. You have a responsibility to know your subject matter, and your students can quickly figure out if you really do or if you need to rely on the review questions at the end of the chapter to "get through a lesson" you don't know much about. One aspect of competence is your ability to let students know your strengths and weaknesses. If a student asks you a question you don't know the answer to, don't fake it. Admit it, then do your research and come in the next day with the answer. Use this experience to inform students about how you went about doing your research to find the answer. You can turn not knowing something into an inspiring life and school lesson.

All three Cs are interrelated and must come out in the first 15 minutes of presenting yourself to your class. Remember that *first impressions are created very quickly.* Begin by letting students know that you care about them. Caring is one of the most powerful forces operating in the classroom. If your students believe you care about them, you can motivate them. If they believe that you don't care about them, most attempts you make to motivate them will be an exercise in futility. The question becomes this: "How can you persuade your students to accept the idea that you care about them?"

A good way to begin is by telling them that you care about them. But, if you do that, you must *immediately* back it up. Although I was there an hour before and after class, you can start with just 15 minutes. Let your students know that if *any* of them need help or just want to talk, you will be there for them. Yes, it's an extra half hour of your time each day, but it speaks volumes about your sincerity. Would a half hour a day be worth plummeting discipline problems and a motivated classroom? Remember that it takes two to stop the vicious cycle. This is the beginning of your part.

The First 15 Minutes

One aspect of good teaching is knowing where you want your class to end up. In educational circles, this is referred to as *backwards planning*. Planning out your first 15 minutes should incorporate the following principles:

1. Ask yourself what information and experiences you want the students to have in that initial time period.

2. From there, work backwards to the point where your students first set eyes on you.

3. Make sure that everything you say is backed up with evidence.

The Element of Surprise

Many teachers' first words are a recitation of their classroom rules. In middle school, teachers have to remember that their students transition through six classes a day, unless they are on a block schedule. If kids hear similar messages every period, they will confirm their belief that school is a boring place. Since the messages they keep hearing concern ways to limit their freedom, they also look at it as a confining environment. This is how many school years begin for kids. They come home. A parent asks, "What did you do in school today?" They reply "nothing," and mean it. This is not a pretty start.

In a typical first class, most teachers quickly get to the class rules. They want to act preemptively. Students hear about rules in every class they walk into on that first day.

Here is your first opportunity to surprise them. Most middle school students don't need to hear, "Raise your hand before you speak" or, "You're not allowed to fight or take stuff that doesn't belong to you" on the first day. *They already know all that.* Imagine how shocking it would be if you were to say, "You've been students for years so you know what the basic rules are. Please follow them." By making a simple statement like this you are giving them instant respect and dignity. You are treating them more like the adults they want to believe they are. Communicate that as you all get to know each other better, the most meaningful rules will emerge. On the first day, surprise them by beginning with your *vision statement* instead of your rules.

If you are like most middle school teachers, you have focused on the immediate: *survival*. You never sat down and created a vision statement. You were probably just following the lead of your own teachers who never opened up the year with a vision statement either. Most of us teach the way we were taught. This next section will guide you through creating your vision statement.

Creating Your Vision

When I teach a course in graduate school, I open up the semester by telling my students exactly what they will be able to do as a result of taking this course. Then I tell them why I'm qualified to teach this course. I give them my academic history as well as my professional and personal history. I believe that it's valuable for students to know that I view my professorial duties from the perspective of a father, a former middle school teacher, and a professor. I tell them why I love the topic of educational psychology and continue explaining why I think the course can provide answers to their educational questions. I point out the areas of possible confusion in the course and encourage them to ask lots of questions.

Many students believe that asking a question is like saying, "I'm the dumbest person in the room and I'm the only one who can't follow what's going on." I quickly point out that they need to listen carefully for a specific sound immediately after asking a question. Right after a student asks a question, the rest of the class will hear the sound *"phew"* coming out of five or ten relieved students who had the same question, but were too afraid to ask it. I literally say, "Don't limit yourself to *intelligent* questions. Good questions can be as simple as, "Huh?" or "Would you please repeat that?" or "I understood everything you just said, but there's a guy in the back who seems confused, so for his sake, would you please repeat that?" It is essential to make your class environment *safe* for students who need your help.

I end my first 15 minutes by telling students that I want everyone to earn an "A" and that it will be essential for them to help each other get through the course. I put students in peer editing groups during class time to evaluate each other's work before it comes to me. This helps both the editor and the student whose work is being edited. We go over the expectations and guidelines so that they are clear. I also let students know that if they score low on an assignment, they can resubmit it to get the grade they want. I let them know that it's in my best interest to help them learn things well so I don't have to keep regrading their papers. Peer editing and resubmission show students that I use assessment to make sure they learn, not as a way to categorize them with grades. This is another way to demonstrate my level of caring.

My First 15 Minutes

In order for your opening segment to work, there are certain things you need to address to present yourself as caring, credible, and competent. After you welcome students to your class, tell them about your academic history. When I introduced myself to middle schoolers, I always included a funny story about middle school. For example, I lived in fear for 180 days of the sixth grade because of "Dump Day." On entering middle school, I was told that Dump Day was the day when eighth graders grab sixth graders and throw them into trash cans. Everyday I used to run from my classroom at lunch to a place that I had heard was the "Safe Zone" on campus. I would end fourth period the same way. I would slowly gather my things up. I would go to the door. I would peer out. Then, like a bolt of lightning, I would make a mad dash to the tree in the corner of the yard. I would then breathe a huge sigh of relief knowing I had made it to the "Safe Zone" again. This happened every day. Later, I learned that Dump Day was just an eighth-grade joke, like snipe hunting. The eighth graders had no intention of throwing me in the trash can. But, they had a great show every day around 12:15. I tell stories like this because they bring us together as teacher and students. We know that people like stories, and middle school students are actually people.

In addition to going over your academic history, it is important to tell students why you enjoy the subject you teach. Tell them why you decided to teach the subject and grade level you currently teach. Did you select it when you were in middle school? I suspect that you probably didn't. If this assumption is correct, remember that few kids in middle school have career aspirations to teach middle school. If you introduced yourself in a way that created a bridge rather than a divide, telling students why you like the subject is just another reason for some of the kids to try to like it as well. Finally, your first 15 minutes should address why the class you teach is relevant for the students *right now*, in today's world. More important, tell students why it is *personally* relevant to them.

I have found several interesting results from this introduction. First, I get feedback from students, early in the semester, letting me know that they feel like they know me and are more comfortable coming to me than other professors who seem more guarded and standoffish. Self-disclosure is a good way to show caring. Second, they tell me that when I talk about my background, it adds to my credibility. Third, they tell me that they believe I'm there to help them learn. These first 15 minutes are a shrewd investment of your time. However, once the students buy in, you *must* live up to your words.

So, your first 15 minutes are over. The students have a sense about *who* you are, *why* you are there, and have been given reasons for why *they* should be there. Congratulations. You have laid the foundation for a successful year. Now the work begins. You have to build on the foundation you created during your first 15 minutes.

Getting to Know You

There is a well-known Hollywood actors' joke. An actor is in a conversation and says, "Well, I've talked enough about myself. What do you think about me?" We know that people love to talk about themselves. However, it's really difficult to show caring about your students if you don't know who they are.

You have given them information about you. Now it's their turn to give you information about them. An effective follow-up activity after your first 15 minutes is to get your students to write about themselves. Ask them to answer the four questions that follow. This data will help you learn who your students are under the best circumstances. We all love to brag, and it's best to brag when you think people are *really* listening and interested. We like people who make us feel good about ourselves. Answering these four questions will put your students into a position whereby they can write down what makes them feel good about themselves, to a caring and interested audience—you!

The Four Questions

1. Until now, *how* have you liked school?

2. What are your special talents and gifts?

3. What do you like to do?

4. What do you want to get from this class besides a good grade?

When you get home that day, get comfortable, take out these papers, and read each one carefully. Make sure you are alert and in a good mood as you do this. If your attention starts to drift, take a break and come back to it. This is the beginning of your chance to bond with each student. Because you are doing this as a written exercise, you give your students a chance to write as much about themselves as they want—in private. Because you are the only person who will see these papers, you can guarantee that their information will be kept confidential. As you are well aware, middle school students become embarrassed very easily around their peers. By doing this, you also gather an informal assessment of their writing abilities. Most important, you develop an understanding about each student and can begin to craft a strategy to captivate each one. These strategies all require you to invest some time, but you will make it up by having fewer classroom management problems.

More Daring Caring

There are many additional ways to demonstrate caring to your kids. One of the most important is to make them feel safe in your class.

Safety First

There are some middle schools where physical safety is a concern. Whether it is fear of one-on-one violence, gang violence, physical bullying, emotional bullying or cyber bullying, these issues need to be addressed. If a student ever contacts you about one of these safety issues, it is essential that you take immediate action. Generally, these are schoolwide issues. They must be addressed all the way from the top administrators to the custodial staff and every point in between. In this section, we are more concerned about students' emotional safety.

There are many ways that kids can feel unsafe in your class. When I was in junior high school back in New York, my math teachers wanted to guarantee that we were stripped of any feelings of safety as we entered the room. The more vulnerable we seemed, the more important it was for them to remove any shreds of dignity we might still have left. I guess they assumed because that strategy worked so well in the military, why not use it here? One of their favorite methods was to select kids who didn't seem to be doing well and ask them to write their work on the board.

I can still remember being called on to put my solutions to math problems on the board. I can still feel the back of my neck turn red as I was writing on the board and hearing kids laughing at my work while my back was turned. I used to wish that I never had to turn around and face the class again. As I did turn around, I would swear that I saw a smirk on the face of my teacher as the kids laughed at my solution. Then, the teacher would ask the class how many of them could see something wrong with my work. I watched all those hands raise. Finally, she would call on one of the better students to actually come up and correct my work. This five-minute experience took about an hour in my mind, a long brutal hour. Her name was Mrs. Allerdice. She's probably no longer with us, but in the unlikely event that she is, I hope somebody shows her this page.

Please keep in mind that your kids are going through a huge transition in middle school. Adults are losing their authority; it is being sapped by students' peers. For students, their peers' impressions of them mean everything. If you put them into a position where they will be embarrassed in front of other students, they will hate your school, your class, and of course, you! So what are some things you can do to increase their feelings of safety around you?

Decreasing Their Fear of Detection

There is an abundance of kids with skill deficits in most urban schools. There is an incredible range of reading abilities in any middle school classroom. Asking kids to read aloud is a great way to embarrass many students, if that is your goal, but sarcasm aside: please avoid doing this. It is embarrassing beyond measure for most kids, and it is also incredibly boring for the rest of your students. They have to sit passively and endure bad, choppy, nervous reading. Their only possible source of entertainment is laughing at the kids who don't read well. They can read silently at twice the rate that they can read aloud. There is no reason for this kind of tortuous task.

It is important to make kids feel comfortable when they are learning something new that is difficult. You already know that they will make many mistakes along the way. You have to let them know that you expect them to make mistakes along the way, that it's part of the process and helps them grow. Alerting them to the common mistakes is a great form of scaffolding. The important thing is to make them feel safe to experiment and learn new skills, even if it is very difficult. It's easy to practice your strengths, but very few people like to practice their weaknesses. Remind them that if they don't go through this process, they may end up like Abdul.

The Story of Abdul

I was one of five new students beginning a karate class. There were four of us who were very raw, unskilled, and awkward. And then, there was Abdul. Abdul was also new to karate, but he was an accomplished soccer player. The way a soccer player kicks a ball is very similar to a roundhouse kick in karate. Abdul could put you through a wall if he hit you with his roundhouse kick. Every time we had to fight in class, we prayed. The teacher would call one student's name and that student would stand up. Then he would call a second name. If he called Abdul's name first, we would shudder, hoping to hear any name but ours next.

Every day we would come to class and practice. We learned front kicks, side kicks, roundhouse kicks, crescent kicks, back kicks, and spinning kicks. We looked liked clods, but we kept practicing them every day, and slowly, we got better at all of the kicks. All of us went through this except Abdul. He felt that he was so far above us that he wasn't willing to look foolish trying all those new kicks. The only thing he worked on was his powerful roundhouse kicks.

After a couple of months, we all couldn't wait to fight with Abdul. We knew what he was going to do because he only had one skill. Pretty soon we were beating him up on a regular basis. We were *hoping* to hear our name called after Abdul. Pretty soon, he got tired of being beaten up and quit.

Practice your weaknesses, not just your strengths.

Being Available

We've already suggested that if you came in 15 minutes early and stayed 15 minutes late, you would be more available to your students. Another way to demonstrate your availability is to give them your e-mail address. E-mail is great because it is very unobtrusive in your life. You can read it and respond to it on your own time schedule. It also maintains your students' privacy. They can talk to you without anyone else around. You'll be surprised how many problems you can avoid in class by making yourself *omni-available.*

Being Approachable

I find that when I question many medical doctors about their choice of treatments, they tend to act defensively. Their attitudes seem to say, "I'm the doctor," and that's all that should be necessary. I find this trait shared by too many teachers as well. I think the Pope has enough problems with being infallible; we don't need this burden as teachers. Ironically, making an occasional mistake ingratiates you to your students. You end up appearing human. It ends up increasing the empathy you share with your students. Here are two ways you can increase your approachability: throw in an occasional mistake that students can catch and correct you on and use self-effacing humor.

Making Mistakes

Occasionally misspelling a word on the board is a great way to offer your class an opportunity to correct you. It's a very public mistake. The key is how you accept their criticism. You want to indicate that you understand you are not perfect and that you don't expect perfection from your students either.

Self-Effacing Humor

Self-effacing humor is another powerful technique to make you accessible to your students. Making fun of yourself shows that you don't take yourself too seriously. We did some research recently where we asked teachers to rate their principals on how they used humor. We found that principals who use hostile forms of humor were judged as unapproachable. Those who used self-effacing humor were judged as more approachable.

If you choose to use self-effacing humor, you must use it correctly. The rule is that you can only kid yourself on areas of strength. If you are big and work out a lot, you can make fun of yourself being weak or working out too much. If you are in bad shape and puny . . . leave the area of strength alone. Self-effacing humor in areas of weakness are perceived as admissions of weakness and make people feel uncomfortable.

Learning Their Names

When I was just in my third year at the university, I was asked to go into a middle school and, in one day, tell the faculty why everything they were doing was wrong and show them that my way was the right way. I was barely 30 years old. I knew I was probably going to be one of the youngest people in the room and that they were going to kill me. I tried to think about tactics to delay their onslaught and decided that I would learn all of their names. You've probably been in situations where you walk into a room and meet 10 or more people. They begin introducing themselves, and by the seventh or eight person, they all laugh as if to say, "Oh yeah, like you're going to remember all of these names." Sometimes they'll even joke about giving you a quiz at the end, because everyone knows you can't remember that many names. My strategy was to go around the table, have the 20 or so people introduce themselves, and remember their names. I thought this would have two great benefits. One, it would make me appear friendly because I was making an effort to know them, and two, it would surprise them. Maybe they would be impressed thinking I was smart and delay my execution for three of four minutes. So, here's how I did it.

Some people might call this cheating, but I considered it a good use of understanding Paired-Associate Learning (Schneider & Bjorklund, 2003). This is the name psychologists give to flash-card type rote learning. There are three stages. One stage is called *Response Availability.* In this case it meant learning all of their names. I asked for a list of the teachers a few days before and had all their names memorized, even though I didn't know who the names belonged to. It's like kids learning the names of the letters from singing the Alphabet Song. They know that there's a letter called "j" even though they don't know what it looks like.

Another stage is called *Stimulus Discrimination.* In this case, it meant learning what each person looks like. I stared at each teacher as he or she entered the room and kept staring until there was something unique that I could remember about each person. If a child is learning letters by appearance, it's easy to tell an "x" from an "o," but it's difficult to tell a "b" from a "d." I learned what each person looked like so that years from now if I run into one of them at a supermarket I will think, "Hey, there's one of those teachers that wanted to kill me."

So, now I knew their names and I knew what they looked like. There was one more stage left: *Stimulus-Response Pairing.* I had to *link* the name with the face. While they were chatting with each other, I tried to listen for any of them to use a name to give me a head start. The real work was trying to pair the name with the face during the actual introductions, but two thirds of the work was already done before I got there. They were impressed. Throughout this book you will learn some of the other survival techniques I used that day. The important thing to take away here is that learning kids' names is another way to prove to them that you really do care.

Involving Parents

The more your students' parents are informed about your class, the more likely you will be to get cooperation from home. There are several ways you can keep parents in the loop. One of the best things you can do is to create a class newsletter. Let parents know what you are doing and what they can do if they want to get involved. You can give them tips on how to work with their kids, fundraising news, and samples of their kids' work. If many of the parents don't speak English, you can create a bilingual newsletter. It will be good practice for your students to do the translating.

If you have a parent community that is technology-enabled, and if you or your students have the skills, you can create a class Web site that parents can access whenever they want. If they are fairly low-tech, you can just send letters home every month or so.

In Closing—and Opening

Remember that your students begin to form their opinion of you before you say a word. Right or wrong, they will evaluate your age, your gender, your ethnicity, your clothes, your attractiveness, your physical build, whether you wear glasses, and a few thousand other variables. This process takes a few seconds. Fortunately, during your honeymoon period, you can shape that first impression. A good way to really understand this process is by remembering the experience of going out on a "blind" date. Remember how quickly you determined whether you were happy, disappointed, or needed more information? It took one or two heartbeats. As a closing thought, remember that words do not convince; actions and follow-through do. Middle school students are as committed to data-driven decision-making as we are; they just look for different forms of data.

2 "This is *Stupid*," or Why Adolescents Quit Trying

As a religious man was walking, he looked up at the heavens and yelled, "Lord, I have been a devout believer and I think I deserve a reward for my life of faithfulness."

Suddenly, the clouds parted and a voice came booming out of the heavens. "You're right, my son. Make a wish and I will grant it."

Once the man got over the shock he said, "Lord, I live in California and I love Hawaii, but I'm afraid to fly. Would you build a bridge from California to Hawaii for me?"

The voice said, "I'm sorry, but I had something much easier in mind. Try another wish, but make it simpler this time."

The man yelled back, "OK, Lord, reveal unto me how I can motivate adolescent students."

The voice said, "Would you like two or four lanes?"

What would you pay to learn the secrets of motivating adolescent children? I was always so sure that if I could just get kids to *want* to learn, the resulting motivation would carry students through any educational task. I really believed that teaching middle school was hard because the students just weren't motivated enough. As a psychologist, I've read lots of books about motivation, and I understood the different motivational theories well enough to pass most of my graduate school classes with pretty good grades. Ironically, it was one of my own teaching experiences that made the workings of motivation clear to me.

Here's how my *real* education began. I walked into a room and found myself surrounded by 30 adults who had all set personal goals for themselves, but they just couldn't reach them. These were goals they swore they *really* wanted. Some wanted to lose weight, some wanted to exercise more, some wanted to learn to play a musical instrument, some wanted to work harder on their careers, and some wanted to back off from their careers. I was in a motivation playground. As the professor, that's what I was presented with as I walked into the first day of my *Psychology of Self Control* class at UCLA. Until that time, I thought I understood how motivation worked pretty well, but this class was really an eye opener for me. Before you read any further, think of a personal goal that you have but just haven't been able to accomplish. It'll help you follow better if you're personally involved.

If you've come up with something, we can return to my motivational epiphany. It was one thing to complain about adolescent students not wanting to follow rules, listen to lectures, do homework, or bow to authority, but these were *motivated* adults I was dealing with. And they were trying to achieve goals they believed would make them happy, but they still couldn't do it. The most common complaint I heard in the room was, "I want to lose weight." That was great for me because in those days, I dealt with tons of weight control issues in my work on a daily basis. My approach was to get people to fill out endless amounts of forms with very important data. I wanted them to keep track of how much they ate, when they ate, what they did both before and after eating, how hungry they were, and so forth. I'm surprised they didn't lose weight just from the amount of writing I had them do. Then, I discovered that I could get all the information I needed just by asking them *one* simple question.

I didn't need all of that paperwork. I didn't have to spend time analyzing mountains of data. I simply had to ask just one question, but it had to be answered in the correct way. I'm embarrassed to tell you how simple that question was, but here it is: "Why do you want to lose weight?" Here's a sample of how these conversations went:

Me: Why do you want to lose weight?

Weight Person 1: 'Cause it's better for my health.

Me: Don't waste your time; you won't stick to it.

Here's another conversation:

Me: Why do you want to lose weight?

Weight Person 2: 'Cause I'll look better in clothes.

Me: Don't waste your time; you won't stick to it.

I learned very quickly that with superficial reasons like these, people will never do the difficult exercising and self-sacrifice it takes to change their lives enough to lose and then maintain their weight. These are *actual* conversations I had with people. Here's another. See if you can tell the difference in this woman's motivation:

Me:	Why do you want to lose weight?
Weight Person 3:	'Cause it's better for my health.
Me:	Don't waste your time; you won't stick to it.
Weight Person 3:	Well, there's sort of another reason. A few weeks ago, I went down to my husband's office and saw his new secretary. She's very slim and attractive (*she began choking up and tears began forming*), and I'm afraid that when he's being intimate with me, he's fantasizing about her.

Once this very *real* reason came out, the pounds practically began melting off her. When do we see people really getting into shape and controlling their weight? The most common times are right after a breakup or a divorce. Why is this? It's because they believe that their weight loss will *change their lives.* Let's say you're in a comfortable marriage and secure about your future, and you know your life at home will be basically the same whether you improve your fitness or not. If you're thinking about joining a gym in these circumstances, don't count on changing. You are not motivated enough to change. So, you have just discovered one of the two driving forces of motivation. *If what you want requires hard work, the goal you're going for really has to be life changing.* If it isn't, you aren't going to do the hard work to get it. The second important aspect of motivation isn't as obvious, but it's just as important.

In that same self-control class, two of the students described themselves as musicians whose goals were to improve their playing. They didn't make their living playing music; they just wanted to become better musicians. They knew that the way to achieve that goal was by practicing longer and harder. John kept saying that he was going to have to practice a lot because he usually didn't see much change when he did practice. Marcellus described himself as a pretty gifted musician, but he just couldn't manage his time well enough to practice enough. Being trained as a scientist, I was in heaven because I had two people with the same problem, but they differed in terms of the assessments they made of their musical abilities, or as I liked to think about it, I had an experimental group and a control group.

In case you are not a fluent speaker of motivation, let me translate what each of the two musicians was really telling me. John said, "I'm not very talented, so even if I do practice, it probably won't do me much good." Marcellus said, "I know that I'll improve *if* I practice, but I have to find the time." Marcellus has a chance because he believes that he is good enough to succeed *if* he practices. Poor John will probably never try very hard because he just doesn't think that success is possible for him. So here is the second driving force of motivation. You have to *believe that you are capable of succeeding* before you will commit the necessary energy to make it happen. Taking personal accountability to complete a particular task is well documented in research (Deci & Ryan, 1985, 1991; Ryan & Deci, 2000).

When your middle school students don't seem very motivated, ask yourself these two important questions:

1. Do they believe that they can succeed if they try?

2. Do they think the payoff for trying hard is worth all of their effort?

While all of this is going on, remind yourself of some of the personal goals you have set and how difficult it is to achieve them. This personal understanding will give you insight and empathy. These two tools will optimize your success in motivating your adolescent students.

The Three Components of Motivation

We don't find motivation books very motivating. They are full of theories that have made our heads hurt in graduate school. This book is a result of our headaches from those motivation books added to years of research and many combined decades of classroom teaching experience. We begin this book with a checklist that may not help your backhand, but it will help you motivate middle school students. Rather than just imitating the techniques and strategies we have included, we want you to *use them with understanding.* Educational psychologist Lee Shulman said that psychological theories work really well until chance intrudes, and *it always does.* When it does, you will be ready for it (Shulman, 1995). Here's a little story that will give you some context for examining motivation in an educational context.

When I first began playing tennis seriously, I found a teacher with a serve that was so fast, it physically scared me when I tried to return it. He demonstrated the serve and then said, "Now you try it." My serve was puny compared to his. I kept trying to hit it harder with the same meager results. He encouraged me by continually yelling, "No, no, that's not it." After a while, I got frustrated and said, "What am I doing wrong?"

He picked up a ball and his racket, hit a booming serve, and said, "You're not doing it like this." He was a star outfielder on our university baseball team and his years of hitting and throwing a baseball directly transferred to serving a tennis ball. He never examined the mechanics of his serve, and more important, he couldn't explain it to me.

I found a new tennis teacher. He was a crusty old guy who could barely walk onto the court carrying his racket. He said, "Let me see you serve." I did, and he didn't laugh at me, so I liked him right away. He said, "Toss the ball out in front of you a little more. That way your body momentum will increase and your serve will be a little harder." Later he taught me to turn my shoulders and use my legs, and soon, I was serving pretty well. This experience of having these two contrasting styles of teaching taught me a lot about the process of teaching. The first teacher expected me to imitate him. The second teacher got me to understand the mechanics of what I was trying to do. I have done this with every part of my tennis game. When I am not hitting the ball well, I have a mental checklist of fundamentals that I go through and invariably, I am not doing something on the list correctly. I have created a task analysis of every tennis stroke and carry that information with me (Desberg & Taylor, 1986). Once I discover what it is, I quickly correct it and my game comes back so well that I can stop cheating my opponent with my scorekeeping. This story illustrates the three components of motivation. It has a student (in this case, me), teachers (in this case, the two very different tennis teachers), and a task (the tennis serve).

Each of these three components is fertile ground for increasing motivation. The *first* deals with who our *students* are and what problems they present both to us and themselves. The *second* deals with you, the *teacher* (and any parents who we hope read this book as well). The *third* component is the way to handle the *tasks* that you will use to motivate your students. As you know, you are in dangerous waters. Until you have completed this first chapter, keep your distance from your students. There's an old saying: "Never raise your hand to a teenager; it leaves your ribs exposed."

We believe that a good way to begin solving a problem is to define it first so that you will know what you are trying to achieve and how to recognize success when you have achieved it. We hope that someday, politicians will try this approach. Here are the three challenges (which we know is the politically correct way of saying "problems") around which we built this book: *students, teachers,* and *tasks.*

Component 1: (Adolescent) Students

We begin by examining issues of adolescent students. To understand where the adolescent is, it helps to know how he got there. Erik Erikson was a developmental psychologist who suggested that people progress through eight stages of development throughout their lives. Elementary-age students (ages 6 to 12) are in the Latency Stage, according to Erikson. He referred to the conflict they try to resolve as being between Industry and Inferiority. They begin to learn the relationship between how hard they work and the satisfaction they receive as a payoff. To really grasp what students go through in this stage, take an academic area such as math and picture a normal bell-shaped curve. The student has to identify where he belongs on that bell-shaped curve. Now simply add a few hundred more curves: one for reading, one for throwing a baseball, one for popularity, one for. . . . Hopefully, you can see the picture forming here.

To add to the confusion, students have to not only figure out where they are on each skill and ability, but they have to do it in context. You might be the best piano player among your friends, but there are two much better players at your school. So by the time they begin middle school, students have developed what they think is a pretty accurate, and fixed, idea of how good they are at almost everything, just as they are hitting adolescence.

Now, as adolescents, they begin defining themselves in terms of the roles they will assume, given their abilities. Given those abilities, they have to figure out what paths are open to them and which are closed off. This will determine whom they select as friends, how hard they try academically, whether they conform to school rules and culture, and many other key aspects of their lives.

As if this wasn't enough, their bodies begin changing, their hormonal structure is getting more intense, and they feel like they are not understood by anyone but their peers. The evaluation of their peers becomes much more important than the evaluation of adults. It is not a surprise that they come to you with problems. This is not a complete list of problems, but there is a great deal of research suggesting that these are some of the most outstanding problems students bring with them as adolescents.

A large proportion of students are working below or far below grade level.

Years ago, two colleagues and I walked into a room crammed full of every eighth-grade math teacher from an underperforming urban school district. I asked what seemed to be the problem and they all started yelling at once. When I asked for one of them to start off, a teacher stood and said, "I have students in my classes who are ready for algebra, and students in the same class who can't add or subtract, and every point in between. I can't teach in a situation like that." The rest of the math teachers in the room looked like bobblehead dolls, nodding their heads up-and-down in agreement. They all agreed that it was impossible to teach a class with students who differed in academic achievement, motivation, language skills, and aptitude.

Reading is another subject in which a significant number of underachieving students turn up in classrooms. According to recent statistics compiled by Reach Out and Read National Center, California ranks 45th among the 50 states with only 22% of fourth graders testing proficient or above on national reading tests. The need for improving reading skills is critical.

Teachers have lower expectations of low achieving students.

There is abundant research showing that teachers don't try as hard when teaching low performing kids (Cooper & Tom, 1984; Good & Brophy, 2003; Kuklinski & Weinstein, 2001). They give up sooner and often end up blaming these students for their failures. One of my colleagues in the Psychology Department told me about James, an African American student who had received a grade of "D" in his statistics class. He told me that James didn't have a very good math background and often asked for his help. He admitted that he did offer his help, but not very generously. He didn't think James had much promise and preferred to help the students he thought would go farther in the field. He gave James very short answers to questions and didn't see any problems with his actions. He believed that he was putting his efforts where they would do the most good. Within a year, James worked on his algebra skills in our university's Learning Assistance Center, retook the class, and got an "A." Within the next six months, he became the statistics tutor for the Psychology Department. I asked James what motivated him to work so hard and he told me that he was really angry about the way his statistics professor treated him. He wanted to prove the teacher wrong. Occasionally, such bad treatment motivates kids, but far more often, it has the effect of discouraging them. They buy into the idea that they don't have ability and should just give up.

Discouraged students generally have low academic self-esteem.

It is not surprising that students who meet with continuous failure in school develop low opinions about their academic abilities (Pintrich & Schunk, 2002). This low academic self-esteem causes low motivation for studying, less effort in school, and a lack of willingness to take any academic risks. Even when they do try, they give up more quickly. It becomes much easier for them to become troublemakers or to become wallpaper in the school so that no one will notice them. I was observing a student teacher who asked a student in her math class to solve a problem in front of the class. The student responded by using what school officials refer to as the "naughty finger." He was immediately sent to the Administration Office. As I was leaving, I overheard this student proudly say, "Did you see me flip off the teacher? Was that cool or what?" You may ask why a student would commit an act that would surely bring him serious problems instead of complying with a simple request like showing his math problem. If you think about it from the student's point of view, his choice was framed very differently. He analyzed the situation like this: "Either way I'm going to get into trouble. It's more fun to flip the teacher off than to show the class how dumb I am in math and have them laugh at me for being a dummy."

Adolescent students have a higher incidence of behavior management problems (Ryan, 2001). The adolescent years cause two very abrupt social changes. Kids become more resentful of authority and much more concerned about the opinions of their peers. There is no more difficult time for teachers to deal with classroom management issues. Parents lament the fact that their adolescent kids no longer want to have talks with them, no longer ask for their help or opinions, and resent every time they think their freedom is curtailed. This is the time that they go through an almost comic paradox. They want to be thought of and treated like adults, but they dislike adults. They cannot enjoy this irony. More important, they believe that adults cannot possibly understand them. What makes all of this worse is that they become totally egocentric and only their viewpoint makes any sense to them. Not bowing to the authority of teachers is often seen as a way to gain the respect of their peers. Unfortunately, teachers often play right into this authority issue by reacting with anger.

Some Additional Common Urban School Problems

There are many other student-related problems found in today's diverse, urban middle schools. Here are a few of the ones that will lead to additional motivational problems.

1. *There is less value given to education in the home.* There are many kids coming into our schools from homes where parents do not see a clear relationship between school success and life success. It is much easier to work with kids whose parents emphasize the importance of education. A friend of mine was a high school teacher who taught a Latino student who was offered a full scholarship to Harvard University. The parents said they wanted their kids to graduate from high school and then go directly to work to help the family. They insisted on turning down the Harvard scholarship. They saw no value in prolonging their kid's education when he could be bringing in money soon. The more my friend tried to persuade the parents, the more adamant they became in their refusal.

2. *There are many language difficulties in today's schools.* My wife inquired about teaching in the elementary school a mile from our house and was refused because she was monolingual (she actually speaks French, which made her a functional monolingual). The

school told her that there were speakers of over 30 languages in the school and that bilingualism was a prerequisite for work there. The number of languages spoken in many schools is one problem; another is the fact that many non-English speakers do not even speak their own language grammatically and can't express themselves well in written form. Motivating kids you can't speak to can become a very difficult task unless you are an enormously skilled mime.

3. *The digital divide describes the reduced access to technology for many poor urban kids.* There is a very heavy demand for kids to acquire technology competence in schools. Those kids who have access to technology only in schools lag far behind their peers with access at home. Furthermore, there is a substantial amount of evidence showing the relationship between income and scholastic achievement. Kids from low-income families are much more likely to need remediation. When they do get access to technology in schools, it is much more likely to be remedial in nature than their more affluent peers who are learning more technology skills.

Although this isn't a complete list of student-centered problems, it's enough to give you a feel for them. It helps set the stage for teacher problems. It also helps set the stage for examining teacher problems.

Component 2: Teachers

It is tempting to think that if we can just change the motivation of the adolescent student, everything will be fine. In this section, we examine the characteristics of secondary school teachers that must be in place for motivational changes to occur.

Students must believe that their teachers care about them. Students will constantly make judgments about your sincerity. Remember George Burns' famous quote, "The secret of acting is sincerity. If you can fake that, you've got it made." This goes double for teachers. This involves getting to know your students personally, inquiring about ongoing issues in their lives, and showing interest in them. One interesting irony is that students appreciate higher standards and greater demands on them, if they believe that it comes from a teacher's caring and concern for their future.

Teachers must be seen as fair by their students. When you take any disciplinary measure with one of your students, you put that student into an interesting position. Should that student blame herself for what happened, or should she blame you? If you have been consistent in the way you treat *all* of your students, your student just might blame herself. But, if you show the slightest bit of inconsistency in the way you treat the students in your class, you make it easy for that student to blame you for persecuting her. When things happen to people, whether they are good or bad, they find a reason to attribute the *cause* of what happened to someone or something (Desberg, Colbert, & Trimble, 1995). Your students can blame themselves or you. Inconsistency makes it easier for them to blame you.

Angelina was a very nice and high achieving seventh grader. One day she walked into class out of breath and late. She apologized to the teacher. Then she explained that her father's car had a flat tire on the way to school. She handed the teacher a note from her father and a credit card receipt from the gas station showing a tire repair. Would you punish her for coming in late? Take a few seconds to actually answer this question. How would you handle it?

Let's assume for the moment you decide that since Angelina rarely comes to school late, and she does have a great excuse *and* documentation for it, you can let it go. The next morning, Antoine shows up late. Antoine has a long history of discipline problems in your class. He tells you his father also had a flat tire and he hands you a note from his father that seems to be written in the style and penmanship of a below grade-level seventh grader. What will you do now? If you punish him, how will your class perceive you in terms of fairness? You are in trouble with either decision you make with Antoine now. It's easy for your students to see your action as one of playing "favorites."

Humanizing Teachers

Teachers get better results when their students see them as people. Many teachers hide behind their roles and reveal little of themselves to their students. This is where personalization comes in. Let them know who you are and then use the traits you reveal to increase the motivation in your classes. Since I am six feet six inches tall, it didn't come as a surprise to my students that I was a basketball player. Most of the discipline problems in my class came from boys, so I set up a system in which any boy who had zero behavior problems in class for a week was invited to play basketball with me on Friday afternoon. I also provided Gatorade and snacks. If a boy misbehaved even once, he was invited to watch but not participate. I made sure to let him know that his slate was wiped clean for the following week. All he had to do to play again was not commit any misbehavior during the next week. It didn't take too long before some misbehaving girls got involved! Soon thereafter, it became an open basketball game, all tied to positive engagement in school.

You don't need to have any special skills that kids will want to share with you. A little self-disclosure goes a very long way. It makes you human and approachable. Distancing yourself from your students makes them less willing to take risks like asking for your help or advice. If you really want to take the concept of humanizing to its highest form, try self-effacing humor.

Self-Effacing Humor

Use self-effacing humor to show students that you are approachable. There are few things that are more effective at breaking down barriers between teachers and students than a teacher's willingness to laugh at himself. Our research on how administrators' use of humor affected teachers' attitudes indicated that administrators who used humor well were judged to be more creative, intelligent, and likable.

If you have a question or are thinking about reporting a mistake you made, would you want to talk to a principal who would be sarcastic and belittle you with humor? Self-effacing humor shows your students that you don't think you are perfect and you recognize your own flaws. It shows that you make mistakes and don't expect perfection from your students.

Embracing Mistakes

Show an attitude that accepts and even encourages mistakes. Kids love video games. In Steven Johnson's book, *Everything Bad Is Good For You: How Today's Popular Culture Is Actually Making Us Smarter* (2006), he points out that video games teach kids more about scientific method than hands-on science lab experiments do. To play today's complicated video games, kids learn to use strategies like *separation* and *control of variables* and *combinatorial logic.* This is the very essence of procedural thinking in science. Kids learn by trial and error, making wild associations, and experimenting. This also leads to many mistakes. Please encourage them to make mistakes and make them feel safe when they do. There may be times when they need to be careful and avoid mistakes. At those times, be clear when telling them what to do; otherwise, let them experiment so they can develop their own problem-solving procedures.

Improving Clarity

Students have a need for order that you can satisfy by being clear. Clarity comes in many forms for your students. The most important one is giving them clear expectations about what you expect from them. This reduction in their uncertainty greatly eases student anxiety. Examine your own clarity of expression. Just because you have said something doesn't mean that your students have understood it. There are many things you can do to make sure that your students do understand you. The easiest thing you can do is create an environment where students feel safe telling you when they don't understand something that you said. Try to convince your students that you want to know when you haven't made something clear so that you can fix it. Tell them not to assume that you have said it so well that it is their fault if they don't get it. Let them know that you want to explain things again if they weren't clear before.

Using Assessment Positively

Assessment is another excellent way to find out if you are being clear. This doesn't mean you have to follow each statement you make with a quiz. Simply questioning your students will show you how clearly your message is getting across. You can make this questioning more interesting by asking students how they can apply what you have just said to their own lives. Putting them into small groups of 2–4 students and having them explain things to one another will make things clearer to your students. Asking them to elaborate on the concept and applying it to their lives is a very effective technique for increasing both interest and retention.

Knowing Your Students

Really motivating teachers know what is going on with the kids in their classes. Effective teachers can tell you which kids are part of which cliques. They know what their kids' interests are and what they dislike. They often stand by the door watching their kids enter the room so they can tell if a student enters in an agitated state. In this way, they can prevent problems by acting proactively.

Collaboration

Collaboration is a key to effective motivation in schools. Knowledge does not have boundaries, but academic departments do. We recognize that science and math can work together seamlessly, but it may be as important to look at the relationship between science and social studies. Today's issues of cloning and stem cells, technology and nutrition, all have serious social and cultural consequences. It's important to collaborate with colleagues in other disciplines to expand kids' thinking. Both math and physics play major roles in music. Psychology and sociology also play key roles in music. Get kids to look for ways to merge and cross-pollinate academic disciplines. We've looked at both student and teacher issues, but there's one more area to examine. What are you asking your kids to do?

Component 3: Tasks

When I taught sixth-grade social studies, I was enthralled by the curriculum. Ancient civilizations fascinated me. Sixth grade is the first time students are introduced to world history. It is their first exposure to conflict between their personal beliefs and a scientific perspective of the origin of man. Students in sixth grade study the dawn of humans all the way up through the rise of the Roman Empire.

One particular unit in the sixth grade focuses on ancient Egypt. My students were very fortunate because I had visited Egypt when I was younger. In fact, I was in the sixth grade during the time of my visit there. I thoroughly enjoyed planning this unit. Throughout the planning process, I remembered places I had been to such as the Great Pyramids at Giza. I was flooded with pleasant memories. I spent weeks planning the lesson that would end with students doing an independent project based on the retelling of my adventures.

The unit flopped miserably. The students were bored senseless. They were rude. I was hurt and angry. I had a stern conversation with the class. Actually, it was more of a scolding than a conversation. I explained that students should respect all the hard work their teacher put into preparing a lesson. The lesson ruined my day. It took me until the drive home to realize what went wrong. First of all, I misunderstood the audience with which I was working. I designed a unit of instruction with *me* as the audience. It wasn't the kids who were bored; it was me who was boring. Second, the kids didn't act inappropriately. They acted precisely as any adult would act if he or she wasn't interested in a presentation. As a teacher, I used to attend professional development workshops. They reached levels of tedium I didn't know existed. Teachers reacted by taking out their newspapers and reading them during the presentations. Some teachers actually slept through the workshops. Our students aren't allowed to sleep. They are expected to look entertained and aware. Kids learn how to manipulate a speaker early. I often reflect on that Egypt lesson as an example of how *not* to teach or plan for instruction. Finally, I vented in the wrong direction. I forgot the most important rule in teaching. It is the teacher's job to make the subject matter interesting to the students, not themselves.

Designing Tasks for Learning

Designing motivating tasks is a tremendous challenge, but it is this challenge that hopefully attracted you to the teaching profession in the first place. When I was a new teacher, the thought of coming up with an exciting way to introduce a topic made me feel like a coach diagramming a great play. Designing good instruction is just like game planning, except that each week you play the same opponent. You will see many examples of how you can introduce lessons throughout this book. As you select among them, there are many factors that you will have to keep in mind.

You have to know your students. You have to know how they learn best, how to read facial expressions and body movements. To design challenging and meaningful tasks, you have to learn how to introduce new concepts in a way that will capture their imaginations. Your introduction to new material should capture their attention. Research in educational psychology clearly suggests that it is essential to have their attention before they can learn and retain any information. You have to have their attention before learning can take place. You want to pique their curiosity. You need to make them *want* to listen. Designing tasks to motivate students has several essential elements.

Relevance and Value

Students will work harder if they see the *relevance* of the task to their lives. This gives the task real *value*. This is where an effective sales pitch comes in handy. Automobile salespeople know what they are selling. Customers know why they come into the car lot. Students are often sold a blind product. They are actually buying the expenditure of their own effort. If they like what you are selling, they will be more willing to work through the challenges that accompany any task. Let's go back to sixth-grade social studies. The likelihood that any student will visit Egypt, China, Israel, Greece, Rome, or Iraq is pretty slim. The likelihood of visiting ancient Greece or Rome is even remoter. Students rarely see themselves becoming writers, historians, or mathematicians. You have to convince them that their career might hinge on a persuasive business letter they may have to write. They have to believe that they may lose a big deal if they can't keep the numbers straight on an important business deal. More important, teachers can't keep saying, "You'll need these skills—someday." Adolescents live in the present. That's why most of this book presents lesson ideas that will affect your students right now.

Cooperative Learning

Having students work in groups is another effective strategy for designing effective tasks. There are certain conditions you must meet for students to work effectively in groups. There must be a *common task* for the group. Group members must be responsible for contributing *independently* toward the final product. Most important, there must be interaction and dialogue. You must determine how much noise is acceptable and productive for your class. There is no set answer here, but there are a few considerations. First is your own tolerance level. If really loud noise levels are jarring to you, even if it helps the students, it isn't worth it if it keeps you in a constant state of upset. It is a good idea to have a noise level where you can get everyone's attention without having to yell. You need to be able to hear what is going on within every group in the room. This is important because there will be times when students within a group will quarrel and you will need to intervene immediately.

There are certain times when putting desks in pods of three or four tables is most effective. There are also times when group work is not necessary and sitting in rows is appropriate. Everything you do in your classroom doesn't have to be collaborative. A motivated classroom has a dynamic interplay of collaboration and friendly competition. You must know your audience.

What is the optimal group size? Research on social loafing (Karau & Williams, 1993) suggests that the more people you have working together, the easier it is for group members to disengage. The ideal size for group-based work is three. With four, critical decisions can result in a draw. With five, it becomes easy for one person to quietly slip under the radar and not contribute. When confusion arises, the "smartest" student usually takes over and ignores the rest of the group. However, size doesn't always matter. To increase the probability that a group will remain motivated and on task, each member's role must be *identifiable* and all group members must be *accountable.* There is a great deal of research demonstrating that when each individual's participation is observable, motivation increases. Throughout this book, you will get strategies on how to keep members of your class accountable.

Selecting Groups

So the stage is set. We will continue to look at students, teachers, and tasks. When you are creating groups, the activity should guide the group selection process. If the assignment calls for specific individual strengths within the group versus the need to group problem solve or do research, your group composition will differ. If you want some kids helping others, it would be a good idea to put high ability and low ability students together. Research suggests that the most effective group rotation period is about once a month. You want students to learn about how the others in the group work, think, interact, and behave. If students need to be grouped by specific skills, you can give every student a multiple intelligence inventory. Depending on the project, you can include a variety of different profiles so that everyone's strength will become realized.

Using Feedback

There is research going back as far as Pavlov suggesting that the optimal amount of time between completing a task and getting feedback is about a half second. You can tolerate way longer intervals because you have the use of language as a basis for your thoughts. As a student, you submitted a paper or homework and often you didn't receive feedback for several days.

Compare that to your students' delay of gratification for feedback. They are frustrated when a Google search takes more than a few seconds. They are used to high-speed Internet connections where they get instant feedback. If they have to use a dial-up account, they can exhibit extreme frustration.

The type and quality of feedback you provide is essential. My former teaching partner did not have a good relationship with his students. He often demeaned them and gave them way too much work to do. He was nice to me. I often told him that if he let his kids know how nice he was, he would get along better with them. He used to regularly give the students upwards of 50 math problems every night. When he graded their work, he opened the teacher's edition of the text and compared the answer in the book with the answer the student wrote. He never analyzed *why* a student was making a mistake. I don't understand why a math teacher would assign even 20 problems for homework. The more homework you give, the more you have to grade, and the less time you have to analyze your students' areas of difficulty. More important, most lessons can be assessed using far fewer problems. If my teaching partner had looked for patterns in his students' thinking, he might have been more effective at reteaching. Sadly, he wasn't an effective teacher. The students resented him and relished the times he was absent. Feedback should be about providing direction rather than criticism. We strongly recommend giving students effective rubrics before starting any project or assignment.

Summary

Interesting things happen on a daily basis at every middle school in this country. Not one middle school goes through a day without a challenge. Students are beaten up physically and mentally. Students get their hearts broken during nutrition and find true love by lunch. Students come to school hungry or sleep deprived. Middle school educators need to remember that one of the keys to motivating adolescents is to continually remind themselves that adolescents *are adolescent.* They make stupid mistakes and they need someone at the school who can build relationships and foster intellectual, interpersonal, and social growth. Many times, a child makes an attempt at crossing the bridge toward adolescence during middle school.

Middle school students try new language or dress differently. Jean Piaget clearly reminds us that adolescents still need concrete examples of learning prior to the introduction of abstract concepts. Motivation theory tells us that students have to choose to engage prior to investing ongoing mental effort. The development of the individual occurs and is nurtured on the grounds of the school. We are by no means arguing that children shouldn't be held accountable for bad behavior, but we are attempting to suggest that adolescents are at a critical individual development point on which teachers *can* have a profound impact, both positively and negatively. When you design your classroom instruction, it is essential to examine the relevance to the lives of the adolescents you are facing.

When I deliver professional development to schools, I often introduce teachers to my mantra of dealing with adolescents. The mantra is simple: "It begins with me . . . it ends with me." By adopting this mantra, I ask teachers to commit to the idea that many times, motivational issues are not about the adolescents but about the inflexibility of the teacher to meet the students at their level and present appropriate challenges to them. Whether it is called scaffolding, differentiated instruction, or tracking, it doesn't matter. Student learning challenges must be owned by the teacher because if the ownership is off-loaded to the student, you will never be able to make appropriate changes to your curriculum, teaching style, or ability to provide meaningful feedback to students.

3 The Classroom Management Toolkit

Classroom *management* systems are wonderful methods to build a classroom culture and keep students motivated. They always focus on student learning. Teachers make shared decisions with their students, and they help students understand how the studied material will be personally relevant to their lives, both now and in the future, in a way that is personally meaningful to them. Anything that approaches classroom rules and maintaining order is framed in a way that relates their classroom behavior to attaining these goals. And there are probably three schools that actually exist like this, although we heard that one of them is slipping over to the dark side.

Classroom *discipline*, on the other hand, begins with an assumption that without rules, there would be anarchy in the classroom. Students need rules to keep them from running amok. As you can see, the discipline approach is not nearly as attractive as the management approach. When you can use the management approach, it is unquestionably preferable. So, why would you ever need a discipline-oriented approach?

The Role of Discipline

When you have a classroom full of truly motivated students, there's no problem, and you will adopt a management-centered approach. Why would you ever need a discipline approach? Let us help you look way deep within yourself for an answer to this question. Imagine you come to a four-way intersection at night. The intersection has these characteristics:

all four streets are straight so you can see clearly for miles, and there are no other cars coming from any direction. Remember that it's night so you could see headlights from quite a distance. The light is red and you have been stopped for a long time. There would be no physical danger if you just ran the red light. So would you ignore the red light and go through the intersection? Most people I ask say, "No," even though running the light would not place them in any danger. When asked why, they say they're afraid of getting a ticket. Even if they don't see a police officer, they are afraid that there may be one lurking in the shadows, or there may be a camera or helicopter or some form of radar. This sounds suspiciously like a discipline-based model to me. Why don't you take more liberties on your income tax, or walk on the grass, or litter? Occasionally, I'm pleased to find an ethical person who doesn't take advantage of these situations on moral and ethical grounds, but more often, most of us conform to rules because of the fear of punishment. A ticket for running a red light brings a large fine, a huge increase in your insurance premium, and if you are really unlucky, traffic school. Most teachers use a mix of discipline and management strategies in their classroom. They have rules to keep order, but they try to relate them to the higher purposes of the class.

The Discipline Toolbox

Teachers only have three tools to use for maintaining order. One is used when their students are doing something the teacher likes; they get a reward. When students are doing something wrong, teachers have two choices. If it is a minor transgression, they can ignore it. If it is a more serious problem, they can punish it. Put this way, it sounds very simple. If it is so simple, then why do so many teachers mess it up? Here are a few of the most common mistakes we see when we observe in many classrooms.

Misusing the Tools

You tell your students to read silently from their textbooks, and they do it. In the minds of most teachers, this is no big deal. The students are just doing what they are supposed to be doing. So how do most teachers respond to their students when they are following directions? They do nothing, or, in slightly clearer terms, they ignore them. Teachers commonly *ignore* the very thing they want.

Now, during silent reading, two kids talk to each other. This is something the teacher doesn't like. How does the teacher respond? She scolds them publicly. She is rewarding these students by having the entire class give them attention.

A student is fooling around instead of doing the math problems he hates to do. The teacher, thinking he is punishing that student, sends him to the teacher next door. Sending him out of the room rewards him by letting him avoid the math he hated doing in the first place. The lesson here is, know what you want and deal with it appropriately. Here is a crash course on using these three tools effectively.

Using Rewards

Most books on classroom management refer to rewards as *reinforcement.* This word is a holdover from the days of behaviorism. That's unfortunate because it merely means using a reward, which we all do. If you are intrinsically motivated to do math, that just means you find doing math problems rewarding or reinforcing on their own merits. Reinforcement can come from within or from the outside. There are students who just love doing math for its own sake and others who love getting good grades for doing math. Furthermore, these two are not mutually exclusive. Some of your students may like both math and good math grades. If you are lucky enough to have students who either like the wisdom they receive in your classes or the grades they bring home to get rewards from their parents, you are lucky and your kids are pretty easy to motivate. Then, there are the others. For them, you must solve two problems:

1. Find out what your students will think is reinforcing.

2. Figure out what to do if your students are not giving you any positive acts to begin reinforcing.

What Students Find Reinforcing

I spoke to a teacher who said, "I tried that reinforcement stuff (the word *stuff* was substituted for the sake of decency) and it doesn't work." I asked what she did and here was her explanation:

> I told my students that if they behaved from Monday through Thursday, they would get to listen to music on Friday. It worked for the first four days so I brought in several of my favorite Debussy recordings and played them for the students, and from that minute on, it no longer worked. Using rewards failed.

In case you are not a serious classical music fan, Debussy was the first major Impressionist composer. For most adults, his music is abstract, lacks melody, and is very intellectually challenging, or in a word, *boring.* To an adolescent student, it would be like listening to 100 musical instruments tuning for 45 minutes. This poor teacher didn't understand that what she thought was reinforcing was actually quite punishing for her students. The important take-away from this story is this: just because you think your students will like something doesn't make it so. By the same token, just because you think you are punishing students doesn't make it so either. We had an eighth-grade teacher who would constantly lose his temper and scream at us. I guess he thought that was punishment for us. We used to walk out of class laughing and saying, "I thought for sure he was going to have a heart attack in class today. Maybe tomorrow." Then we'd laugh some more. We didn't really wish him any harm, but it was fun for us to make him scream and turn purple.

So, how can you find out what will actually reinforce your students? Here are two quick strategies: ask them, or observe them and see what they do when given a free choice. Now, here is an even better idea: do both of those things. Then, offer them a choice based on your listening and observation. By offering them a choice, you are directly involving them and showing them that their needs are important to you. Another advantage of giving them a choice is that it guarantees that you can deliver on any choice they make. It's a little tough when you ask a student what she wants and she says, "A pony."

Offer students choices that are already part of the regular school environment. You don't have to bring in candy and stuff. They would be very happy to have the opportunity to decide who to sit next to, which group they will be part of, what topic they get to study next, what activity to do next, and so forth. These choices will not disrupt the flow of your classes.

Finding Something to Reward

What if they don't give you anything to reward? There are times when you can stare at a student for hours waiting for a nice, cooperative act and receive nothing. This is tough when you want to use rewards, but there are two commonly used techniques to handle this situation.

Observational Learning

If your student is giving you nothing to reward, find a neighboring student doing the right thing and praise that student, making sure that your troublesome student notices. This way he learns that he can get a reward just by doing the right thing. Make sure that the reward is accompanied by a clear verbal explanation of why the student is being rewarded. There is a classical story of a teacher walking down the hall of a middle school when a student suddenly holds up a knife at her menacingly.

Without missing a beat, she looks at the student next to him and says, "I like the way you're not pulling a knife on me."

Shaping

Instead of waiting until a difficult student does exactly what you want, look for a small step in the right direction. Then keep rewarding successive steps that get closer and closer to the one you want. Psychologist Ivar Lovaas (2002) pioneered the use of this technique with autistic children.

Ignoring (Extinguishing Your Students)

Psychologists refer to ignoring as the process of *extinction*. It literally means to stop rewarding something that you used to reward. The idea of extinguishing troublesome students sounds very inviting, doesn't it? There are two important issues you must clarify before trying extinction. First, is the infraction you are dealing with a good candidate for extinction? It must be something that is in no way harmful to anyone. It should be a minor annoyance, nothing more serious. Then, you must be the source of the reward. If a student clowns around in class and all the students laugh to maintain the clowning, you are powerless to extinguish it because you are not the one rewarding it.

Understanding Punishment

Imagine that one of your students wants to talk to a classmate, but there is a rule prohibiting talking during class. While your back is turned, you hear the sound of whispering. You wheel around quickly and catch these two students whispering to each other. You caught them red-handed and you sentence each of them to detention after school. What are the results of this scene that gets played throughout classrooms everywhere? First, these two students have now learned not to like talking to each other anymore. No, that doesn't sound right, does it? So what have they learned? They've learned not to get caught. They will develop more clever techniques such as waiting until you are otherwise engaged, or texting each other, sending notes, and so forth. Have they learned anything else? Yes; they've learned that you will punish them when they do something you don't like. You are to be feared.

If punishment produces so many negative results, then why do people use it? Psychologists have the answer to that simple question: *Punishment is fun for the punisher.* My former teaching partner was a tragic example of this. He would seemingly relish "going O-F-F" on students, as he used to say. Of all the ways to change behavior, punishment is the only one that will give you *immediate* results. The results may be short-lived, and the students you are punishing may grow to hate you for it, but the effect is *immediate.* We don't get to see the carnage until later; some never notice it. When my teaching partner was absent, the room became tranquil and serene. They hated and feared him. The price is often bad attitudes, dislike of the teacher (aka punisher), and even dislike for the environment in which it's given—school. So how does punishment actually work?

Immediate but Short-Lived Effects

The first thing that we know about the result of using punishment is that it works best when it is initially used. Then, after a while, students get used to it and it loses its effectiveness. Students often learn to ignore it. So the effects of punishment soon get weaker. Things like "time out" and scolding seem to work when you first use them, but you've probably noticed that once your students get used to them, they seem to lose their effectiveness fairly quickly. If you want to continue using them, you have to keep making the punishment more intense. To get the same effect, you have to become much more severe. You don't want to be a teacher who is placed in the role of having to make punishments more severe to maintain order.

Types of Punishment

There are basically two forms of punishment: (1) presenting something bad and (2) taking away something good. An example of presenting something bad is verbal abuse, such as shaming a child or embarrassing her. Time out is an example of taking away something good because you are removing a student from an environment that he enjoys such as talking to the girl next to him. If you are going to use one form or the other, *taking away something good generally does less harm.* It is much less likely to leave emotional scars.

The Best Form of Punishment

Psychologist Alfred Adler was one of Sigmund Freud's original disciples, and he was one of the first psychologists to study the use and effectiveness of punishment with kids. He said that the environment has a way of punishing kids that is more effective than anything teachers can come up with. He advised using the *natural consequences* of the environment to punish children. For example, if your child is late and misses the school bus, he has to walk to school. If a student lies to you and then later wants something, explain why she is now untrustworthy and can't get what she wants. Adler's basic premise was that the stove would teach the child about HOT using a naturally occurring form of punishment. The environment rarely makes mistakes the way people do. You will never hear a student say, "That stove just doesn't like me."

The Real Value of Punishment

Although a mild form of punishment doesn't produce long-lasting results, it does have some valuable functions. At first it works and it is immediate. This is the time to introduce an *alternative* response. Remember at the beginning of this section on punishment, you saw that punishment doesn't alter the motivation for wanting to do something, only what you will do to get it. Your students will not learn to stop wanting to talk to each other because you punish them for it. But, if you punish them for talking, then they will stop talking at first. This becomes an opportunity for you to introduce an alternative response that can permit their talking, with your blessing. This is what they wanted in the first place. You can tell them that *if* they complete an assignment in an allotted time, *then* they can talk. Or, if they perform a task, they can be in the same cooperative group and work together. Even though the effects of mild punishment aren't long-lasting, they work long enough for you to show your students an easier way to get what they want that is more in line with the way you want your students to act.

An Incompatible Alternative Response

The best way to use alternative responses is to introduce an *incompatible alternative response.* You have a student who is bigger and stronger than most of the other students in your class and he enjoys bullying them. Create a job in class like, "fight monitor." It is the fight monitor's job to break up fights, write up a short report, and take the guilty students to the assistant principal's office. Make sure to give this student recognition by saying something like this:

> Billy is going to assume the role of "fight monitor." I'm picking Billy because he is the biggest, toughest, and meanest student in class and no one is going to fight as long as Billy's the "fight monitor."

Billy is now getting the kind of attention he wants, and he is in a role that is *incompatible* with his former behavior. Instead of getting his parents called in as punishment, his parents are getting letters home that praise his cooperation in class. If he wanted to fight now, he would lose his new position. Kids that are sloppy can be put in charge of cleaning up. Students who are lazy about completing assignments can be put in charge of keeping work records. You are limited here only by your imagination.

Rules: The Heart of Discipline

There is abundant research pointing out that students like to feel safe and have a minimal amount of uncertainty in their classrooms (Palincsar, 1998, Rogoff, 1998). Even when they choose to break the rules, they like to know the nature of the risk they are running. With this in mind, here is the king of rules: *be consistent!* It sounds so simple to say and so difficult to do. In life there are usually two sets of rules: the *stated* rules and the *real* ones. If you are driving down a state highway with a posted speed limit of 65 mph, do you always stay at that speed or below? If you observe most drivers on the rare occasion when a highway is clear enough for them to drive at the speed of their choice, they very rarely drive at 65 mph or less. At what speed do you feel comfortable driving when there is a posted speed of 65 mph? Most people will drive at 70 mph without the slightest fear even if a Highway Patrol car is behind them. How did they arrive at this comfort level? They arrived at it through testing and observation. Years ago, the Highway Patrol in California went out on strike. People went out to freeways in the desert and were driving at well over 100 mph when there was no risk of getting a ticket.

We all test rules to see how far we can bend them. The more inconsistent you are in following up on your own rules with consequences, the more you are inviting your students to test you. If you tell your students to be in their seats by class time and a student is a minute late, and nothing happens, one of them will have to find out if two minutes will work. If it does, how will three minutes be dealt with? If you crack down on three minutes on some occasions and not on others, then you have made the game more tantalizing. How can you get around this? Here are a few principles to follow that will lower the chance of your students having to test you:

- *Set very few rules.* Then you don't have to spend a lot of your time policing your class and having students see you in that role. It is easier to be consistent if you don't have as many rules to be consistent about. Students will feel less confined if there are fewer rules. This will also keep the resentment level toward you much lower. Make sure that you discuss the relationship of those rules to achieving the goals of your class and how they provide a safe environment for your students.
- *State the rules very clearly.* Make sure that it is very clear when rules are being followed and equally clear when they are not. Setting rules clearly avoids arguments about whether a rule was actually violated. It makes the students' decisions to violate rules very clear, which in turn makes it easier for them to accept the consequences of their actions.

- *Be consistent and eliminate exceptions.* If your rules are stated well, you will be able to apply them equally across the board. For example, there will have to be a rule about tardiness. Students often come to school late with legitimate reasons for being late. There are times when their tardiness was clearly not under their control. You will be placed in a horrible position if you have to make the decision about whether to act on those cases. Instead, create sane rules and consequences. It is not reasonable to expect that in the course of 180 school days a student will *never* be late. Determine how many times it is reasonable for a student to be late. If it's three, then you can hold students accountable for *any* tardies after the third one. If students are late twice with great excuses, they are held accountable but not punished.

Classroom Discipline, Management, and Perception

Regardless of the management system you institute in your class, it is still you who is establishing and maintaining it. Whatever goes on in your class will always be a reflection of you and your attitude toward teaching and your students. Throughout this book, we discuss the importance of establishing a caring relationship with your students. There is no stronger reflection of your attitude toward students than the way you establish and sustain your classroom environment. *Classroom discipline* is essential, but it is better if it is done within the context of *classroom management.* Classroom management is essential but still better if you follow some basic principles of *impression management.* The way you handle classroom climate is probably the single most important message to students about your attitude toward them. Filter every decision you make in terms of how you want to be perceived. This does not mean that you want to sacrifice order for popularity.

Mr. Steirs was my eighth-grade homeroom teacher. He told lots of jokes and was generally considered a good guy by the students. If you came to class a few minutes late, he just made a joke about it and went on with whatever he was doing. He was also my history teacher and he had the same attitude in history. Occasionally, a few students would talk to one another in class, then a few more would do it and before we knew it, he was only lecturing to three or four students out of a class of 35. On the average of three or four times a month, he would seriously lose his temper and scream at the class. He would say how hurt or angry, depending on the day, he was with us. He would then threaten to get very strict, but he would ultimately go back to his old ways. We liked him, but his inconsistency was just too tempting for eighth graders to resist. And it's always fun to see teachers yelling.

There is a great deal of evidence that students like teachers who set high expectations for them (Good & Brophy, 2003; Stipek, 2002). Students are concerned that they are treated with respect and caring. You should never lower your standards or excuse misbehavior to curry favor with your class. It has the opposite effect. It would make you appear weak and uncaring. You can approach maintaining your classroom in the same way that business people go into a business partnership. Each enters into the agreement and makes a commitment to abide by that agreement or face the consequences. Consistency is next to Godliness, if you have a very small dictionary.

While we are confident that traditional theory in educational psychology provides a clear base from which to analyze problems and challenges, we also have real-life teaching experience. A healthy blend of these two perspectives will enable you to better address challenges, both as they happen and before they happen. Understanding the role of punishment and rewards is critical, but effective teachers have both proactive and reactive tools on which to rely.

From Band-Aids to Tourniquets

In case of emergency, break the glass and read this!

In karate class, as we'd be catching our breath after a grueling activity, our teacher would offer us some of his wisdom. Here's a typical sample: *(You have to imagine this said in a heavy Korean accent if you want to soak up the full flavor. It would help to run in place hard first so that you are panting and trying to catch your breath as you are listening.)* "If you near someone who angry, move back a step or two away so he no can sucker punch you." Then he would follow this or any other advice he gave with his favorite tagline: "Remember, an ounce prevention worth a pound cure." Although it loses something in the translation from those intense moments, he had a way of making us believe that his advice could end up being the difference between life and death.

In our view, an ounce is not nearly enough prevention; we'd like tons of it. Don't ever make the most dangerous mistake a new, or veteran, teacher can make. Don't assume that your students will like and respect you just *because you are the teacher*. There are certain preventative steps you can put into place to reduce the likelihood of problems in your classroom. It doesn't matter who you are or how much your students like you. At some point in your teaching career, a crisis will reveal its ugly head just to see your reaction. A crisis might be something as simple as a playful eraser fight in your GATE World History course, or, it might be way more severe, like a gang fight erupting in your classroom. As you will see here, *an ounce of prevention is worth at least a pound of cure.* Don't do anything rash until you have a firm grasp on the following pages. It could save your career.

Preventing Classroom Chaos

There are four essential steps every school needs to embrace. Planning for all of these steps should take you no longer than 75 minutes, but failing to do so could cost you untold hours of frustration and anguish.

Step 1: Set up your rules and consequences.

This step is better thought of as *the most obvious step in the world.*

- *Post your rules where they are visible to every student.* Every rule you set must be enforceable. Remember, there are schoolwide rules and there are classroom rules. Make sure they are compatible.
- *Be sure that your rules are absolutely clear to every student.* "Treat others as you expect to be treated" is not a rule, it's a motto. A rule is an objective and clear description of classroom behavior that is expected at all times. Here is an example of a clear rule: "Profanity of any kind is not permitted." If your rules are unclear, students must try to clarify them by trying out all of their edges to see how far they can go. Don't give them the opportunity to have that much fun at your expense. If your students try to get cute about seeing how far they can push the profanity rule, give them this rule of thumb: "If you have a question about the word, it's profanity."

Step 2: Get your administrator's consent.

After you complete setting up your rules and consequences, walk a hard copy to the principal, assistant principal, or dean, and anyone else who is part of the discipline team at your school. Ask them to sign a copy to show that they have seen the rules.

- *They do not have to approve of your rules, but you should obtain a signature so they commit to supporting your efforts.* If they have any objections, they will voice them at this time, long before you need their support. If they say nothing and sign, then you have gotten their consent. This makes it much easier to count on them later.
- *The earlier this gets to the administrative/disciplinary team, the easier it will be to get their attention.* It's easier for them to sign your rules in the abstract. Once there is a loud child or parent screaming, some administrators may back down. Before school starts, everyone is calm.

Send a copy of your rules home to your students' parents. There might come a time in your semester that you need to get the administration and the parents together for a conference about a student.

Note: Middle school students are not the best paper returners. Consider having every student fill out a self-addressed, stamped envelope and mail your introductory letter and classroom behavioral guidelines home. You will greatly increase the response rate of these guidelines.

Step 3: Explain the concept of choice to your students.

Once your rules are posted, point out to students that the basic laws of cause and effect are in force. If a student puts his hand on a hot stove, the stove does not *decide* to burn the student based on how much the stove likes or dislikes him. That's what stoves do. It is the student's decision to put a hand on the stove and test to see if he gets burned, but once the hand is there, the time for decisions is over. There's only one consequence and the stove has specified it. Once a student is tardy, hits another student, or doesn't turn in homework, you, as the teacher, have no decision to make. The rules have been set up to take care of it. Your job is merely to be consistent so that every student is aware of what will happen when a rule is broken. Your other job is to remind your students of this both verbally, and of course, through your consistency. Then, your job is to become a stove.

Step 4: Create a detailed record-keeping system for classroom management.

When I taught middle school, I kept a metal index card box on my desk. Over the years, I would add stickers to the box and the edges gradually became dented and bruised. When I would open the box, and it was not often, the creak from the hinge would draw the attention of a few students. Inside the box were three things: alphabetized card sorters, blank index cards, and index cards with comments on them. If you followed my rules, this box was not a source of anxiety for you. For those daring souls who challenged the classroom code, their familiarity with the box was a source of fear.

- *Every teacher must maintain a clear record-keeping system.* Mine was in a metal box. Of course, now it would be a plastic box with cables and chips. When a student broke a classroom rule, I would document the event carefully. Each card had the date when the rule was broken, what the student did in detail, and the consequence that was applied. It was not quite as nice as a database, but for its time, it served me well.

I wouldn't interrupt the class when I had to make a comment, but I carried a clipboard or a small pad in my pocket that I would scribble on. Later that afternoon or evening I would complete cards for the students who violated classroom expectations. I did this after school because some of the consequences required parental phone calls and this made the entire process more time efficient.

Crisis Management

You have taken all of the preventative steps you could have taken, and yet, it still happens. A crisis occurs. Experts in classroom management (Emmer & Gerwels, 2002; Emmer & Stough, 2001) have identified procedures for handling inappropriate behavior. Following are the steps you can take to handle it:

Isolate the Problem

The first thing you must do is to isolate the individual who is at the root of the problem. Isolating the offending student(s) will offer safety and protection to the rest of your class and keep the problem from escalating. This will give you additional time to think through your alternative courses of action without worrying about the security of your students. Before you can resolve any conflict, you must first define the problem, and you want to do this with as little stress on you as possible. Here are a series of strategies that will help you get control of the situation and reinstitute a sense of calm and focus:

- *Use proximity strategies with the student.* There are several reasons why moving closer is helpful. Confronting, negotiating, or correcting a student from across the room increases your chance of failure. Putting a student in a fishbowl so that the entire class is now looking at her will make it much more likely that the student will become defiant, defensive, or hostile. She will be a lot more willing to listen to reason and back down if it can be done privately. It is also helpful to move closer to a student and, nonverbally, indicate the alternative behavior you would prefer.
- *Use verbal inclusion strategies by using the name of the offender in your dialogue with the class.* Be careful not to humiliate the student, but you want to involve the offending student to show your class that you are aware of her misbehavior. For example, if you saw a student texting, it would be better to say, "Joanie, please remember that we don't text during group work," then saying, "Remember class, we don't text during group work."

- *Ask the student if she is aware of how her actions affect learning or share how her behavior makes you feel.* It is wise to incorporate "I" statements rather than focusing on the students' behavior. "I" statements let your class know how *you* interpret *their* behavior. When you say something like, "You don't show any respect in class," to your students, it is interpreted as an accusation. If your students do respect you, they will feel misunderstood, if you are lucky. They will become hostile if you are not so lucky. It would be better to express the same thought like this: "When you talk during my lecture, I feel like you are not showing me any respect."
- *In a quiet, nonconfrontational manner, ask the misbehaving student to state the rule or procedure that was broken and encourage her to follow it.* Sometimes a problem can be solved with a simple reminder. It is always better when you don't have to resort to punishing students.
- *In a firm, nonthreatening tone, tell the student to cease the maladaptive behavior.* Here again, a clear verbal direction may get a student back on track. Always try to use the least restrictive alternative first. You can always ramp things up later if necessary.
- *Use motivation, which centers on individual choice.* Give the student a choice: "Stop throwing things across the room or you will be sent out of the room." This is an easy way to remind the student that she is "choosing" to have something bad happen as a consequence of an undesirable act. Referring to the cause-and-effect nature of the situation may get students to rethink their actions.

At this point, you have isolated the student, used your existing signal to get students' attention, physically stood near the offending student to end her negative behavior, and maybe even raised your voice a little for emphasis. If your classroom is still not under your control to the extent that you want it to be, we now consider taking more drastic measures.

Using Human Resources

In most television shows for children, the main characters attend school as part of the program. Shows like *Jimmy Neutron, That's So Raven, Fairly OddParents, The Suite Life of Zack and Cody,* and *Hannah Montana* use school as a frequent setting. This is great for you because your students are already prepared for the next step. They know that when kids get into serious trouble, they're going to be sent to the office. The strategy of sending problem students to the dean or the principal was around when Socrates sent Plato to the principal's office when he was a student in middle school.

Removing a student from the class accomplishes two things. First, it stops the problem immediately. When you remove the trigger, other students instantly see that you intend to have an orderly and safe classroom. It also enables you to work through the problem with the remaining students in a calmer manner. If you send a student to the office, follow these strategies:

- *When you write the referral, be specific about what the student did.* Nothing annoys a dean more than receiving a behavioral referral that's vague. It's difficult for an administrator to support you if he doesn't know why a student is sitting in his office.
- *Indicate what outcome you would like to see on the referral.* Do you want the student suspended? Do you want a parent conference? Would you like the parents to come in and sit in on their child's class?
- *Keep your own documentation of each student's misbehaviors.* If you find that there is a need for a Student Study Team, your referrals and documentation become evidence of the types of interventions you have already used.
- *Never get personal with the student.* If you feel the need to remove a student from a learning environment, make certain you are addressing the behavior of the student and not the student himself. Adolescents still have a difficult time separating criticism from personal attacks. They love to say, "He just doesn't like me," or, "We have a personality clash." Classroom removal is a public display. Use a great deal of thought about the language you use with the student in front of the entire class. Remember that you will be seeing this student again, and the audience is listening, wondering how you will treat them.
- *Have a fellow student, but not a friend, escort the student to the dean's office.* You must be selective about who you choose. If you have a teacher's aide (TA), use this invaluable resource. Often, the student will tell the TA and the dean why he misbehaved. Sadly, the student usually states that the teacher triggered the behavior. Document, document, document—this will protect you.
- *Make it a point to follow up with the dean.* Most deans are faced with a heavy caseload and usually don't have time to sit and craft a thoughtful, eloquent response to the referral notice. Always keep a copy of the referral note with the dean's comments on it. It serves as a receipt of sorts in case the behavior continues. Here's a valuable little tip. Bring some coffee to the dean's office and have a quick chat. We're told that deans like Krispy Kreme doughnuts, but that may just be an urban legend.

Schoolwide Classroom Management

For a very brief period of time, I helped out my middle school by serving as interim dean of students. It was strange being the campus bad guy (even though you really aren't the true bad guy). What was strange was that I would see teacher frustration clearly on each referral slip. Teachers would often write words like "defiant," "rude," or "uncooperative." Many times, these referral slips would be accompanied by phrases like "suspend for 2 days." As dean, I would read the referral slip and look quizzically at the student. In as straightforward a manner as I have, I would ask the alleged violator to tell me exactly what she did because it wasn't clear on the form. In many cases, the student would honestly have no idea what she did that warranted being removed from the classroom. Of course, there were cases where kids wouldn't say anything, basically admitting some guilt. As I consider myself to be a fairly approachable guy, I would take them at their word, unless I had reason not to, and I would talk to them about the qualities of being an effective student. After about 10 minutes, and a threat or two, I would write, "Counseled and returned to class," and send them on their way back to receive instruction.

Many times, those five words would trigger unexpected anger from the teachers. They would rush at me and demand to know why those students weren't suspended and why they were returned to class. My answer was simple. If I didn't know what they really did, how could I take such an extreme measure? I often retell a version of this story in my professional development seminars with teachers and they all laugh knowingly. They recognize that the need for clear, consistent communication is essential. After all, the base of all communication is getting what you need out of an interaction. Without clarity, confusion breeds and anger soon follows. There are two things to take away from this story that all teachers need to know. First, use the dean or assistant principal as a last resort. When you send a student out of a classroom, you are doing two things: (1) you are causing a student to miss your dynamic, valuable instruction; and, (2) you are informing the remainder of the class that you are not the final authority. Furthermore, you are giving away your authority to someone who usually doesn't know the student as well as you do. Solve as many problems as you can within your own classroom. If you have to refer a student, be as clear as possible and detail what the student did so the result will not only provide an immediate remedy to your classroom, but it will provide the student with a learning experience he understands and internalizes. I recently spent three hours at a high school reading referral slips. I would have sent 90% of them back due to lack of clarity. While the student might have been horribly disrespectful, all I could conclude was that the teacher didn't have basic classroom management skills or was a poor deliverer of instruction. Some teachers actually wrote, "Suspend per Ed Code." This was laughable because there was no evidence describing what the student did. This leads nicely to why schoolwide policies must be consistent and institutionalized.

Every school has a faculty handbook that includes a lot of essential information such as emergency drill procedures, school maps, sample lesson plans, and substitute request forms. One glaring omission I continue to see at many of the schools where I consult is a guide for referrals. As an organizational system, it is critical for everyone to clearly understand exactly what can cause someone to be removed from instruction. This should either be in the form of a checkbox on a referral form or listed clearly in the faculty and student handbooks. These reasons should be identified and agreed to collectively as a faculty because every school will have unique differences and needs. In Los Angeles, I primarily work with urban schools and we collaborate to develop appropriate campuswide discipline policies. The guidelines at every school are different because threats facing students are different at each school. That said, there are certain constants at every school that should result in removal from a classroom. These include, but are not limited to, the following:

- Fighting in the classroom
- Striking or threatening to strike a teacher or other staff member
- Using drugs or appearing to be under the influence of a controlled substance
- Harassing or sexually abusing other students or teachers

Each school also has unique challenges, and as a faculty, you must discuss them openly and honestly to determine what "your list" will look like. More important, everyone must follow these guidelines. Once you have generated a list and agreed to follow it, the information must be clearly disseminated to your faculty, students, and parents. The more transparent you are, the more support your plan will receive.

In addition to having a mandatory removal list, your school faculty should agree collectively to actions that should *not* result in removal from a classroom. The list that follows contains actual reasons for removing a student from the classroom. I have personally seen every one of them and, as you can tell, these are issues all teachers should be expected to handle in their own classroom. Here is the list:

- Chewing gum
- Sitting in gum
- Laughing at a joke that wasn't funny (not racial or inappropriate, just not funny)

- Farting
- Not bringing a pencil to class
- Not bringing a book (or other supplies) to class

Effective schools collaborate and make serious attempts at being consistent and professional. With regard to campuswide discipline systems, we believe that these strategies provide an appropriate jumping-off point to have meaningful discussions with your colleagues. Keep this thought in mind as you think about student behavior expectations. The students transition multiple times throughout each day. They have to adjust to different rules, expectations, and teacher demeanor, not to mention all the challenges of being an adolescent in the 21st century.

It's Good to Have Friends

You don't have to turn to administrators every time you want a student out of your class. It's a great idea to make a deal with neighboring teachers, particularly the ones who are great at managing their classes, to exchange students when necessary. Make sure that you have talked this over in advance so you can do it at a moment's notice.

It's advisable to handle a situation before it goes too far. The sooner you deal with it, the less momentum gets built up and the easier it is to manage. If you notice a student refusing to follow a simple request or not following directions, it makes everyone's life easier to have that student complete the work in a different environment, like a neighboring classroom. Here's a word of caution. Make sure the room you are sending the student to is under control, quiet, and *not* a room the misbehaving student enjoys. If you send the student to her favorite teacher, she may increase her bad behavior because your consequence turns out to be a reward for her.

Connecting With Parents

Sometimes you will believe that you are following all the rules, doing everything right, and just not getting results. This is a good time to look homeward. Very often, your student comes from a home environment that is vastly different than your classroom. In many cases, this can be an individual difference. For example, there are homes where kids are princes and princesses. They get catered to and receive attention whenever they want. Others kids get almost no attention and have to create a crisis to get noticed. To complicate matters more, if your school is urban, or rural, chances are that you have students coming from vastly different cultures.

When I was interning as a psychologist, I ran a group at the university counseling center. One day a woman who was born in Los Angeles to Japanese immigrant parents told the group about an incident. She was married to a white man who came home drunk the night before. As she was putting his shirt in the hamper, she noticed lipstick on his collar, and on closer examination, she smelled perfume as well. She confronted him about it and he began hitting her to the point where she came in with visible bruises.

When she told her story, the group, consisting of mostly women, was outraged. They offered her the names of divorce attorneys and told her to separate from her husband immediately. She began to cry and explained to the group that by growing up in Japanese culture, she was taught that it was the woman's responsibility to keep the marriage together. She went to her mother to ask for advice and she suggested that she crawl back to him on her hands and knees and beg for forgiveness. Next, she went to her brother expecting more understanding because he was brought up in the United States like her as a Japanese American. He told her to take a sex class and learn how to better please her man. She told the group that she understood their outrage, but she was caught between two cultures and still believed that it was her job to keep the marriage working. The women in the group left feeling very exasperated because they just couldn't understand her point of view. As you can see, others' cultural views can be baffling, even when we know about them, and maddening when we don't.

So what can you do when your rules just don't seem to be working? It's a good idea to consult with your student's family. If you can see that there are clear cultural differences, find out how you and the family can work together to structure a management system together. Here is another example. As you read it, imagine how differently it would have turned out if the teacher had taken the time to get a brief cultural education first.

One of my students was teaching in New Mexico in a local public school near a reservation. The students in her class were each given a poem and told they had a week to memorize it and then recite it to the class. A Native American student in her class refused to recite the poem. The teacher threatened him with suspension if he didn't. He got suspended for defiance. He would not follow the teacher's rules. His father, a village leader, was outraged and insisted on a face-to-face meeting with the teacher. He explained that in their culture, presentation was valued highly and members were encouraged to perfect a presentation before giving it because of its importance. He explained that his son was practicing it constantly to make it perfect. Daily, he spent hours working on phrasing, body gestures, and facial expressions so that he could get the maximum impact and make it worth the other students' time to hear it. The father then called his son over and asked him to recite the poem. The son rattled it off flawlessly, clearly showing that he knew it. The teacher was deeply embarrassed, apologized profusely, and learned the same lesson we hope you do.

Fights

The ultimate nightmare for any teacher is having a fight break out in the classroom. With increased diversity and mounting racial tension and gang membership, fights can quickly get out of hand and have very disastrous effects for the participants and sometimes the innocent bystanders as well. If a fight does occur in your room, get help—*immediately*. Use your phone, send a student out, whatever is necessary, but get some backup right away.

As a large man, I didn't have a problem stepping into the middle of a fight and separating students. But, I still always called for help first. You must exercise caution and remember where your primary responsibility lies. You must always look after the safety of your students first. Make it a point to know your campus policy for these kinds of situations so you act in accordance with them. You must act quickly and decisively.

Every classroom in this country should be equipped with a phone. This phone should have the capability of dialing outside lines as well as immediately connecting you to several critical stations such as campus security, dean, counselor, nurse, front office, custodian, and so forth. Unfortunately, there are many classrooms that do not have working phone lines. Long before any trouble starts, you should have tested your room's phone. Your best strategy in the case of a serious problem is to call for immediate assistance from anyone you can reach. Once you reach one of these people, help should be on the way quickly. Every teacher should also have a cell phone with emergency numbers programmed in it. With two clicks, you should be able to get help.

Calling for help is the correct first step, but now you must take some action until help arrives. Here is a sound suggestion. Create a loud sound. You can scream the word "STOP!" at the top of your lungs. *(Read the "Yelling Story" that follows for a bit of inspiration.)* Or, you can take a chair or trash can and slam it on the ground. Sometimes, if you're lucky, the fighting students will get startled and stop. If they do not, DON'T try to stop them yourself by getting in the middle and trying to physically separate them. There are a number of things that can happen, and they are almost all bad. One or both students may hit you. Or, you may hurt one of them and lose your job, and get sued. The best thing you can do if your students keep fighting is to keep yelling and making distracting noises until help arrives.

The next question is, what should you do with these students?

Generally, your students will get suspended or expelled. If they get expelled, you don't have to worry about them anymore. If you are going to suspend a student, make sure that a parent will be home with the student all the time for supervision. When I was a student teacher, I had a behavioral challenge in the classroom. My master teacher, Doris Davis, who was a fantastic master teacher, asked what I wanted to do with a child who misbehaved with the intention of making me look foolish. I eagerly suggested he be suspended for two days to think about the consequences of this behavior, and I suspended him. Here's what happened. This student's parents were at work during his suspension. On both days he came directly in front of my classroom door and rode his skateboard back-and-forth on the street, screaming at me. It was the last student I ever suspended.

The better alternative would have been to bring one of his parents into the classroom and require an in-school suspension until the parent arrives. That way the student would have been supervised the entire time. In many states, if a child misbehaves in a serious manner, schools can force parents to leave work and be docked pay to accompany their child in a classroom.

The Postfight Analysis

After the class has ended and you have gone home to reflect, think about creating a plan about what you are going to do the next day. You need to regain control of your classroom. Your students will be curious to know what happened to their classmates. Telling them will help you regain some of that control. If the students were suspended or expelled, that is a warning to other students about what may happen to them if they act similarly. Follow this up with advice for students who find themselves in a difficult situation such as being bullied. Let them know how they can contact you privately and what you may be able to do to help them. You can give them tips on what to do if students distract them when they are working and so forth. This is another form of prevention.

Structured Reflection

As you sit down to reflect on what happened, here is a template for you to use. It will help you identify the critical components that are necessary to reduce the likelihood of similar events occurring later on.

Identify what happened in the classroom that day. Be specific. Try to include as many details as possible because they may give you insight into what caused the problem and what you may be able to do about it.

- *Determine how the actions of the student related to your classroom rules and their stated consequences.* Be clear about which rule the student broke and how his actions influenced the flow of events in the classroom.

- *Identify what happened immediately before the event.* This often gives you insight about what triggered the problem. It is a good idea to talk to a few students who were near the event to find out what they remembered about how it came about.
- *Identify what happened immediately after the event.* This may give you insight about what rewards the student may have gotten for doing what he did. For example, if everyone around laughed at something he said, you have a pretty powerful cue. If you make this process a ritual, you might just find a pattern of behavior with that student. Is the student consistently misbehaving *after* group rotation? Does the student come with materials *at the beginning* of class? Look for patterns. By looking for patterns, you can determine whether this is an isolated event or part of a broader pattern.
- *Create a contract between the student, parents, principal, and teacher.* We strongly advocate the use of written contracts between student and teacher (and parent and administrator). By generating a clear contract, with explicitly written consequences, and sharing it with all parties, two things happen:

  1. The student is aware of the consequences that may act as a deterrent for misbehavior.
  2. If the student still breaks the contract, you are not the "bad guy" who punishes the student. It is clear to that student that he *chose* the consequence by committing the act.

Research shows that if you want to build intrinsic motivation in your classroom, you must have structure long before students can be given any autonomy (Pintrich & Schunk, 2002). Adolescents say they dislike structure and authority, and this is true to a degree. However, their comfort increases when they walk into a situation where there are no surprises. Above all, students always want to know that they are safe. Don't worry if you are in the middle of a school year. Any of these strategies can be incorporated at any point during the year. However, they do work best when beginning a new semester.

We leave this section with an inspirational story about how my mentor teacher used yelling as a motivational device.

A *Yelling* Story

Screaming "SHUT UP!!!" in a loud, firm voice is a great way to get the attention of a class during a crisis situation. I have never been a big fan of yelling. Kids don't like yelling either. When you teach, you are on stage all day long. You need to have a controlled authoritative voice that you can call on when needed. At the high end of that controlled voice is yelling. My favorite story about classroom management was one that involved a veteran teacher yelling during my second year of teaching:

> A teacher next door to me seemed to be having a meltdown of epic proportions. She screamed at her students for what seemed like 10 minutes. Her class became disorderly and it sounded like she went nuts. She didn't just scream, she began kicking things around the room. I was stunned, and so were my students.
>
> After the bell rang, I walked across the hall where this woman, who it turned out was my mentor teacher, was laughing. I was still a bit shaken. Her tirade was loud and I'm sure everyone in our hallway heard it. She looked at me and said, "We all yell and throw fits occasionally. You need to remember two things to maintain your sanity and the respect of the kids. One, never make it personal. Two, plan your tirade ahead of time and script what you are going to say so that it works for you."
>
> She said that a $20 investment in her own steel wastebasket can was invaluable. It was a crucial disciplinary tool. She said, "Each year I buy a new steel wastebasket. Sometime during the first week of school, I plant a candy wrapper, or some other trash, near the wastebasket. Then I go through my morning routine. Then comes the big surprise. I notice the piece of trash I planted. I always wear the steel-toed army boots that I bought to use on this one day each year. Then I begin to scream, "Who left trash on my floor?" Then, I begin to kick the wastebasket around the room for about five minutes, screaming as I kick it. All the other teachers knew it was coming, but my students didn't. I am sure my kids thought I was insane, but my room was clean and my students were very careful.

Someday, you might want to raise your voice to get your students' attention. If you choose to do this, make sure you have a specific goal and a plan to achieve it. It is way too common for teachers to yell at a class when their emotions get the best of them. At this point, teachers are not under control. At these times, it becomes very challenging to filter language. You run the risk of insulting your students. Remember, "An ounce of prevention is worth a pound of cure."

Summary

I have consulted at many schools where arguments broke out over whether kids who forgot to bring supplies should be suspended. They could easily have kept extra supplies in their rooms and had a system of "payback for borrowing." Instead, kids are routinely sent out of classrooms every day because they didn't bring pencils. *Discipline tempered by mercy* would be a good start, but *discipline tempered by sanity* would be even better.

A school discipline policy is really designed to breed conformity. If you want conformity, it's critical for you to develop a clear sense of your school identity and value system. Expectations should not differ from room to room and teacher to teacher. Fundamentally, every student should know what the schoolwide expectations are and what consequences await offenders. For example, if you pull a fire alarm at school, you should expect suspension. If you don't do your homework or forget to bring your supplies, does that warrant a suspension from the classroom? There are some teachers and administrators who think so, and some sane ones who don't.

Anita Woolfolk (2008) developed an inventory that analyzes teacher efficacy and routinely finds that the most challenging aspect of teaching, especially for new teachers, is classroom management. This is no surprise. The solution to the problem of classroom management is to be clear, compelling, and fair. What you do to one, you must do to all. If you fail to enforce policy consistently, you lose credibility with your students. I have seen this happen too many times with teachers, parents, and principals. This chapter presents examples, stories, and guidelines to help point you in the right direction. We shared the importance of the first 15 minutes and mentioned in earlier chapters that the real work begins after the foundation is laid. Inconsistency and unfair treatment of adolescents is analogous to lighting a Roman candle in the Malibu hillsides in August—an inferno.

4 What We Know About Learning

Teaching and Learning

Have you ever been to a great lecture? Think about one that was life changing and magical for you. These kinds of lectures usually last at least an hour. So, you've been to this transformative lecture. You were hanging on every word, nodding your head up-and-down, and smiling with each example; it was perfect and you were genuinely moved. The next day, you called your closest friend to share all of the wisdom you had just been given. How long did it take you to retell this extraordinary lecture? If you are like most of us, it took you less than five enthusiastic minutes. So what happened to the other 55 spellbinding minutes you sat through? Remember, this was a life-changing experience for you. What happened is referred to as *information attrition*, a fancy way of saying information loss, or forgetting. You don't remember most of what you heard, even though you hung on every word.

Now, imagine how long it would take you to retell a really boring lecture in which you had absolutely no interest. Add an intercom interrupting the lecture, people walking by the door and making noise, and you worrying about what your peers are saying about you and your friends. You have just entered the world of the adolescent student. As teachers, we really do want to have our students learn a lot and remember what went on during those long years of secondary school. There are two kinds of things we would like students to remember. Psychologists refer to them as *declarative knowledge* (information you remember—like definitions or historical facts) and *procedural knowledge* (strategies and procedures you learn to execute—like math computations or problem-solving routines). There are two main obstacles in getting students to learn; the first is that they usually aren't motivated, as you saw in the previous section on motivation. The second is that teachers often teach as if they know nothing about how students learn. Learning is an active process. The best way to get students to learn is by getting them actively involved in tasks so they will remember. This book is built around a series of these kinds of active learning tasks. Before going any farther, let's just clear up why *you* forgot so much of that inspirational speech that you tried to tell your friend about. It was largely due to the limitations of your *working memory*.

Working Memory

Working memory does not physically exist. Instead of being a physiological brain structure, it's a description of two kinds of events that take place when you learn and remember things. One of them is called *short-term memory*. Information you place there has a very short shelf life. Picture this: You're on your way to the market. As you reach the door to leave, I yell out a list of things I want you to bring back for me. I say, "Bring back some spinach, provolone cheese, pine nuts, 2% milk, a box of Cheerios, broccoli, an avocado, some detergent, doggie treats. . . ." By the time I got to "broccoli," you're thinking, "shopping list." You can only remember about seven items and then you've hit your limit unless you move to pencil and paper. It may be a few items more or less, but for most folks, it's about seven items. You know how uncomfortable you become when someone tells you her phone number and you can't write it down so you're forced to remember it. It's a good reminder of the small capacity of short-term memory (Driscoll, 2005). The second event that occurs in working memory is what we psychologists technically refer to as *thinking*. With all this going on, working memory is where you have to sort through information, decide if it's worth keeping, and then find a way to transfer it into your *long-term memory*. Working memory is the *bottleneck* of the thinking process. You have a limited capacity for a short duration. Try this mental math experiment: Without using a paper and pencil or calculator, divide 34798 by 63. Look at the numbers and then cover up the problem before you begin doing the math so that the whole problem will be done in your head. Go on and give it a try, a serious one. When you've tried it, continue reading, but don't cheat. Really try to do it in your head.

What you probably noticed was that even if you could successfully divide 347 by 63, you forgot the rest of the problem and couldn't continue. Working memory is very limited; information stored there decays quickly (< 30 seconds). Think of the number of times you were introduced to someone new. If you didn't pay close attention to his name and do something to remember it, a minute later it had totally vanished. It actually vanished in only 20–30 seconds. To have remembered it, you would have had to repeat it a few times, or you would have had to form an association with it or used some other memory trick; otherwise, it was transferred into the ozone layer (Anderson, 2005).

Many years ago I walked into a stand-up comedy club and saw a note posted on the wall that said, "No pads-and-pencils or tape recorders please!!!" I thought it was one of the most ridiculous things I had ever seen. I knew they posted the note to protect the comedians' material, but if I wanted their jokes, I could just *remember* them. As I was walking out of the club after the show, I was aware that I'd laughed all night, but could only remember one or two jokes. I'm sure you've had the experience of being at a party where a group of people kept telling one joke after another. You laughed, and you probably even told yourself to remember some of the jokes because they were so funny. But at the end of the evening, you were lucky if you remembered any of them at all. And, if you did, it was probably the last joke or two that you heard. Why is that? To remember a joke, you'd have to go over it in your mind a few times to get it into your long-term memory. But while at the comedy club, you didn't have time to do this, because if you tried to go over a joke, you would have missed the next joke. And you didn't want that to happen. So, you paid attention to each new joke, at the expense of not remembering most of them. The limit on working memory is under 30 seconds.

I took a few classes in college where I understood everything the instructor said. I took notes, but I never went over them. Why should I? I understood everything so well. I would wait until the night before the exam, pull out my notes, then scratch my head and say, "I know that's my handwriting, but I swear I've never seen this stuff before." Even though the information was clear as the professor was saying it, I didn't have the time to process it and place it into long-term memory. If I had, while I was processing it, I would have missed the next thing he was talking about. Furthermore, even if you can actually get something into long-term memory, that doesn't mean that you have access to it any time you want it. To be able to find information that you want, you need to have it well organized in long-term memory.

The Effects of Organization on Long-Term Memory

Here is a confession: I am not a NASCAR fan. It feels almost un-American, but I feel better now that it's out in the open. I have tried to watch a few races on TV and they rarely kept my interest for more than a minute or two unless there was a fiery crash. The cars just seem to go around in a circle making an endless left turn. If I watched five NASCAR races and later described what I saw, they would all be indistinguishable from one another based on my description of them. Since I don't really understand NASCAR, I don't know what to look for. My lack of understanding inhibits the retention of what I just saw. If a NASCAR mechanic were sitting next to me, his memory of it would be entirely different. He'd remember tons of details and would describe a chess game played at 200 mph. On the other hand, I love tennis. I can watch a match and describe the strategy each player is using at any moment in time, the kind of spin on each ball, the pattern of their serves, and much, much more. I remember a lot after I have watched a match because I have a way to organize that information due to my prior knowledge about tennis. I can do the same for boxing and basketball. The more I know about something, the better I can organize new information coming in about it. The better I can organize information, the better chance I have of recalling it when I want it. The better I can organize information, the more *hooks* I have to hang the information on and find it later. The more *prior knowledge* I have, the more I can understand new information. And, the better I understand it, the more efficiently I can organize it. This means I can find it when I need it.

Psychologist John Anderson (2005) has a wonderful analogy to show how organization affects memory. He says that your memory is like a dark attic where your only source of illumination is a flashlight that gives off a very narrow beam of light. I know some people who are very organized. If I went into their attics, I'm sure I would find every 10 years of National Geographic magazines tied together with twine, next to some books that are neatly categorized. Next would be clothing, stored by season, from dark-to-light colors. Even with a narrow flashlight beam, I could find anything I was looking for. I also know some people who just fling things into their attics with the thought that someday they intend to straighten things up in there. When they really need to find something up there, even a floodlight wouldn't be enough light to help them find it.

Here's an important fact: *organization occurs at input*. When you first get new information, you either recognize patterns in it or you don't. If you do, you store the information using those patterns. This will make the information much more accessible to you when you want to retrieve it. If you don't recognize the pattern, the information might as well contain no pattern at all. So, the way you *first* encounter new information determines how well you will store it.

Here's an example revisited. As you're walking out the door again, I give you the following shopping list to remember: eggs, lettuce, tomatoes, sugar, cabbage, milk, flour, carrots, light bulbs, and chocolate. That's a 10-item list and would really stretch the limits on your short-term memory. But, as you were first placing it into your memory, if you said to yourself, "Eggs, sugar, milk, flour, and chocolate are the ingredients for baking a chocolate cake, and lettuce, tomatoes, cabbage, and carrots are the vegetables we use to make our special salad, your 10-item list just became a three-item list: cake, salad, and light bulbs, but only if you recognized those simple patterns at *input*, or, when you were first given the list to place into your memory.

Do you know the difference between students who are smart and "smartless"? There is considerable research showing that the difference is how students use organization when they are learning new information. The very brightest kids will look for organization. If they don't find it, they will create it. For example, during the 1940s and 1950s, phonics was not taught in schools. The brightest kids, who not surprisingly were the best readers, figured out the alphabetic principle on their own and used it to sound out words, even though they were not taught to do it. They figured out phonics on their own. If you tell the next brightest group that there is an organizational scheme to the information they are receiving, they will search until they find it and then use it to learn and remember it. The group under them has to be shown where the organization is, and then they will use it. Unfortunately, with the bottom group, you can show them the organization and they still won't be able to use it.

Teaching *for* Learning

There are basically only two ways to teach. You can tell them (aka deductive teaching—better known as lecturing), or let them figure it out (aka inductive teaching—better known as discovery learning or constructivist teaching). Which is better? That's a silly question. They both have advantages and disadvantages. What's important is using each one correctly so that you make use of what we know about how people learn. Lecturing works fine, if you're a good lecturer. This means you've got to be a good storyteller and know how to weave your content into your stories. The biggest drawback with lecturing, as you've already seen, is the fact that your students are passive during the lecture, and learning is an active process. If I'm a passenger, I can be driven to the same place time after time, but I usually don't remember how to get there by myself. Once I have to drive there on my own, I always remember how to get there again. If you like to lecture, all is not lost. Every 10 minutes or so, stop and give students a short task to do to actively consolidate the information you've presented. You can ask them to write down how the information impacts their life, or put them into small groups and have them discuss it. The key is to have them *do* something with the information so that it becomes better organized. Applying something to your life is one of the best ways to organize information. There are many example of how to do this in the section dealing with *Quick-Thinks* that you'll get to in a few short pages.

If you give students an active task to do, make sure that you structure that task to maximize their organization of the information involved. You can do it by having students discover an organizational scheme of the information and discuss it or by having them relate it to their personal lives. Structure the activity so that students use or acquire the procedural knowledge they need to perform the task. For example, if you had students creating historical newsletters, they would have to know how to acquire information, write a news article, research historical events, and be able to lay out a newsletter on the computer.

The Learning Checklist

There are really three things you need to be aware of when checking your teaching to help students learn:

- ❒ Give them well-structured learning tasks using scaffolding strategies.
- ❒ Provide adequate processing time for students to process and transfer the information using Quick-Thinks.
- ❒ Help them organize the information to make the transfer and storage of information more efficient.

Well-Structured Learning Tasks Through Scaffolding

There are many ways to structure learning tasks to improve learning. In the trade, we refer to this structuring as *scaffolding* (Wood, Bruner, & Ross, 1976). I once heard a description of scaffolding I really liked. It was referred to as *learning with trainer wheels*. When you see a building going up, the buildings are surrounded by scaffolds that are used as temporary supports. You always get rid of scaffolds when you're done, but they sure help in the building process. Everyone accepts the fact that they are designed to be *temporary*. In learning, they help students connect their prior knowledge to incoming information. Scaffolded activities should be just beyond the level of what the students can do alone and then help them to complete this more difficult task that they couldn't have completed alone. If you want to know more about the theory underlying scaffolding, read the work of Lev Vygotsky (1962). Below are some forms of effective scaffolding you can incorporate. You don't need to use all of them every time you teach something new. Look at them as a menu from which to choose appropriate techniques for a given learning task you want your students to perform.

Scaffolding Strategies: Step-by-Step Directions

Students often get stuck in the middle of a lesson. They just sit in class not knowing what to do next. When you are teaching a task requiring the use of procedural learning, it is very useful for students to have a roadmap so they are always aware of the next step. Giving them a set of directions goes a long way toward eliminating student uncertainty. It also helps pinpoint exactly where students are having difficulty so you can zero in on any problems they are having.

Step 1: Provide relevant activities.

An essential part of motivation is demonstrating to students how an activity will directly affect their lives. Make sure you provide a rationale or purpose statement for the activity, showing how it can change, or better yet, improve your students' lives. In many cases, you can structure an activity where students get to choose a task to insure personal relevance.

Step 2: Clearly define learning objectives.

Students like to know what they are going to be able to do after an assignment. They also like to know how they will be evaluated on it. A clear objective helps keep your instruction moving in the right direction. This helps avoid rambling, meandering, wandering, drifting, roaming, diverging, or swerving away from the topic and introducing extraneous information that may confuse your students.

Step 3: Clearly communicate assessments and rubrics.

If I give you a writing assignment and you know that I will be checking to see if your topic sentence sets up each new paragraph, that a transition segues to each new paragraph, and that the document is internally consistent along with your conclusion, chances are, that's what you'll write. If I say, "Write an essay on Bolivia," I am asking for trouble. Educational psychologists refer to these open-ended questions as *ill-defined* (Bruning, Schraw, Norby, & Ronning, 2004; Davidson & Sternberg, 2003). You can probably infer from the term that it isn't the best way to give an assignment. Students, like people, feel uncomfortable with great deals of uncertainty. Providing clear assessment guidelines and rubrics reduces uncertainty and guides students' work with less anxiety. A better way to reach deeper understanding might be to subdivide the class into groups based on interest. One group could create a storyboard of the political history of Bolivia. A second group could create a physical, political, and topographical map of Bolivia. A third could evaluate the customs and traditions of Bolivian people. The more specific the task, the better it is, and the lower the frustration resulting from confusion.

Rubrics let the students know exactly how you will be grading their work. It helps them structure their efforts. This increases the likelihood that they will perform the tasks in the way that you would like.

Step 4: Provide feedback and clarification.

I had a karate teacher who would say, "Everybody practice 500 straight punches." Then he would sit down in his office and read the newspaper. I saw him lose a lot of students, including me. Later, I found a teacher who watched every move I made and let me know when I did something correctly, or he corrected my mistakes. I learned a lot more from him, and I stayed for quite a while. I would like to use one of those straight punches on my first teacher.

Step 5: Use prompts or hints.

When students are having difficulty or get a problem wrong, don't tell them the correct answer. Give them suggestions about things they can try, but then get them to use this new information to solve the problem. Present as little information as you have to and get them to work it out. The more they struggle through it, the more they will learn. The more you give them in the way of help, the more dependent they will become on you.

Step 6: Relate new information to relevant prior knowledge.

One of the keys to organizing new information efficiently is to relate it to what you already know. The trick here is not to just review old information but to review its organizational structure and show how it connects to the new information.

Step 7: Present a list of relevant resources.

When you are teaching research strategies, it's a good idea for students to learn where to find the resources they need. In most other cases, it's a good idea to point students toward the information they need. It's a good form of modeling and a way to make your instruction much more time effective. Furthermore, with all of the sources we would like students to avoid, presenting them with a list of preferred resources is a very safe and effective way to structure instruction.

Examples of Successful Tasks

Another way to reduce task uncertainty is to show students examples of well-done projects. If you are going to do this, try to present a variety of solutions so that students don't begin to think that there is only one way to perform a task. Pointing out what aspects of the project were particularly good gives them even more guidance in terms of creating a good project themselves.

Present examples of common mistakes to avoid.

If you have been teaching for a while, you can generally list all of the common mistakes students will make on any given task. Although it's fun to wait until they make those mistakes and then try to turn their papers red with corrections, it doesn't feel quite as good to the students. Pointing out common mistakes is one of the most efficient ways to guide student work. It also helps clarify the tasks and saves students a great deal of time. In addition, it also saves you a lot of time. If they have to create the mistakes, you have to correct them, then they have to redo the task and you have to regrade it. I'm getting tired just writing about this seemingly endless cycle of pain.

Model procedures.

Sometimes, depending on the task, it is useful to model what you want the students to do. You can do it yourself, have a student who already has the skills do it, or get any student to try it and provide feedback for the group.

Use "think alouds."

This is a form of modeling where the teacher models how an expert would approach the problem the students have been given. He mirrors the strategies and analyses that an expert would go through aloud so that the students can follow along with the path he takes toward solving the problem.

Follow scaffolding with cooperative learning tasks.

Once you have successfully scaffolded the instruction, it is very useful for students to be placed into cooperative learning groups where they can talk through the information you have provided and paraphrase it in their own language so they get to fully grasp it.

Scaffolding provides many advantages. It minimizes student frustration. Students who aren't getting it don't stop learning and feel stuck, or worse; they don't feel stupid. Scaffolding empowers students by increasing their sense of self-efficacy. As they believe more in their own abilities, their motivation increases. They are willing to try new tasks and take larger risks. As you see from the previous list of scaffolding strategies, they engage students in active learning situations rather than getting them to be passive lecture listeners.

Adequate Processing Time Using Quick-Thinks

Scaffolding was the first item in your learning checklist. The next one to focus on is making sure you provide processing time for your students. If you lecture, which is an excellent teaching device if you lecture well and are interesting, you need to switch from straight lecturing to *interactive lectures*. Research provides a great deal of information about the interactive lecture (see Cooper, Robinson, & Ball, 2003; Johnston, 2003; Johnston & Cooper, 1997; MacGregor, Cooper, Smith, & Robinson, 2000). These authors recommend using many of the scaffolding techniques mentioned earlier, and they encourage lecturers to insert Quick-Thinks.

Knowing that attention spans of adolescent students is fairly short, every 10–15 minutes insert a Quick-Think into your lecture. This involves asking a question that students will either respond to in writing individually or talk through in small groups. Quick-Thinks provide a comprehension check, but more important, they provide an opportunity for the students to process the information at a deeper level and make it easier to transfer it to long-term memory. Following are a series of Quick-Thinks which researchers have identified that can provide your students with the processing tasks that will further their learning and retention. There is a great deal of evidence showing that simple repetition of information does not produce deep learning or long retention. Instead, students should be engaged in elaborative rehearsal (Cassady, 1999; O'Reilly, Symons, & MacLatchy-Gaudet, 1998; Terry, 2006). Elaborative rehearsal asks students to incorporate information into their thinking so that they integrate it with their prior knowledge and act on it with their previously stored skills. As you read through this list of Quick-Thinks, you will immediately see how they will lead to a deeper level of processing than listening to a lecture ever could.

Select the best response.

A problem is presented along with some solutions and students must select the best one for the situation.

Correct the error.

The teacher presents information to the students, including some information that does not fit or is inaccurate. The students must correct the statements.

Complete a sentence starter.

The students are given a sentence stem, and they must complete the sentence in their own words to demonstrate that they understand the information presented.

Compare or contrast.

The lecture stops and the students are given two theorists, theories, or concepts, and they are asked to cite similarities or differences between them.

Reorder the steps.

Given a procedural learning concept, students are given a series of steps in randomized order and they have to reorder them to make sense out of them.

Support a statement.

The instructor presents a statement and students must identify the support for that statement from the lecture material just presented. It is a very effective way for students to synthesize information.

Reach a conclusion.

Given a series of facts, principles, or concepts, students have to come up with a logical conclusion that makes sense of the information presented to them.

Paraphrase the idea.

Students take the idea presented by the instructor and put it into their own words.

Organizing Information

The final item in your learning checklist is improving the organization of incoming information. David Ausebel (1968) talked about the use of *advance organizers.* If you have ever read a textbook, you are familiar with summaries that repeat content at the end of the chapter to help you remember the most important facts. In some texts, similar information is also placed at the beginning of a chapter. These are NOT advance organizers because they deal with content rather than organization. Advance organizers tell you how the information you will be reading is organized rather than what that key information is. There are two very useful kinds of organizers. *Comparative organizers* are used when you have some appropriate prior knowledge. They activate that knowledge so that the new information will be easily assimilated into what you already know. Have you ever heard of a sport called Team Handball?

I had never heard of Team Handball when I got a phone call from a musician friend of mine who was also a sports fanatic. He was very excited and said that they were about to launch a professional Team Handball League and he was asked if he would like to compose the league anthem. He was calling me to see if I wanted to help write the song for the new league. I said I would love to, but I had no idea what Team Handball was. I remember seeing people play handball in schoolyards when I was a kid. They wore leather gloves and hit these hard little rubber balls with their hands, and I imagined a bunch of guys in uniforms hitting these little balls. I called another friend who had a physical education degree and asked him if he knew anything about Team Handball.

He described it as a game played on a wooden floor with a ball midway between the size of a volleyball and a basketball. You moved the ball across the floor by dribbling it, just as in basketball, and then when you got down to your opponent's goal area, you tried to get it into a net, past a goalie, just like in soccer or hockey. Because I was so familiar with the other sports he named, I quickly understood Team Handball. My friend used a great comparative organizer to get me to understand the concept. Sometimes, there will be occasions where you will be speaking to an audience that may not have the prior knowledge necessary to relate to your content. In this case, you would use an *expository organizer.*

An expository organizer provides the organizational structure of your presentation rather than presenting the content. For example, if I was called on to present a lecture on the issue of abortion, I might begin it this way: "Today I am going to be talking about abortion. I will begin by presenting the two opposing positions: pro choice and pro life. I will then define both sides of the issue. Then, I will give a series of arguments used by the proponents of each side. Next I will present the counterarguments given by both sides. I will conclude by discussing the political implications of both sides." Notice that I did not present the content of the talk. At any time during my talk, listeners will know which section I am in and how it relates to the other sides.

Another interesting way to show organization is through the use of concept mapping. Although you can have students create a concept map with a pencil and paper, there are many pieces of software that make this task very easy. The best-known software tool is called *Inspiration.* There is an elementary version of the software called *Kidspiration,* and there is a program that lets students plot data in a very visual way called *InspireData.* All are available for free trials versions at www.inspiration.com.

The End of Learning

If I had just finished reading this section on learning that you have just finished, my head would be reeling right now because there was just way too much information—presented without much opportunity to practice it. Here's what I would do with it, as I'm hoping you will too. From time to time I would reread it, looking for new techniques to infuse into my teaching. I would try to work in examples from my own teaching so that each concept would make more sense to me. Even though we have presented some examples, they aren't nearly as valuable as your own examples will be.

5 What We Know About Motivation

Motivation is easy to define; it's the force that guides behavior from beginning to end. There are lots of other definitions of motivation (Festinger, 1957; Ford, 1995; Freud, 1966; Hull, 1951, 1952; McClelland, Koestner, & Weinberger, 1989; Mowrer, 1960; Rogers, 1963; Schachter, 1964; Thorndike, 1913; Tolman, 1932), but we like this one because it works *by definition.* If you smoke and then get motivated to quit, you will quit. If you don't quit, you weren't *really* motivated. It's what philosophers call a *circular definition.* It's only motivating *if it works.* If you're motivated to lose weight or learn to speak Spanish or improve your backhand, you'll do it, or you weren't motivated enough. So, defining motivation isn't very difficult, but there are two difficulties we face whenever we are dealing with motivation: motivating ourselves and motivating others. The rest is easy. Psychologists like psychological theories. They create them, criticize each other's versions of them, and make their students learn them. We like motivational theories for a different reason. They can help guide us toward creating systematic motivational change in our students. We have selected a theory of motivation that is elegant in its simplicity and powerful in its results. It's the one we think explains why your students behave the way they do and how you can change all that.

The easiest way to talk about motivation is by breaking it apart. In other words, it rarely helps a student if a couple of teachers get together and just say, "The kid isn't motivated." It's just too ambiguous of a statement and doesn't give you any idea about what to fix. Here is the theory we find most useful.

Expectancy-Value

When we think of student learning, and we are trying to figure out how to motivate students, Expectancy-Value theory provides the best frame of reference (Eccles & Wigfield, 2001; Wigfield & Eccles, 1992, 2000). Expectancy refers to how likely you believe you are to succeed at the task. Value refers to the desirability of success and how much you want it. It is a very useful theory to describe the motivation of middle school students. If both factors are high, you are increasing the likelihood of having a motivated group of middle schoolers. If either is not, there is little motivation. It gives the teacher a roadmap for generating meaningful lessons.

Expectancy is a student's prediction for her success on any specific task (Pintrich, 1989, 1999). Students' assessments can be affected by how intelligent they believe they are, how difficult they think a task is, and three or four thousand other factors, such as how well they slept the night before, whether they took their medication, whether their friends from a previous class remembered to tell them enough of the answers from the test they just took, and so forth.

Value refers to how much students care about a task (Wigfield & Eccles, 1992, 2000). If we tell you to read Chapter 4 and answer the five review questions that follow, and you are a pretty good reader, your expectation for success might be high. But, if the chapter is really boring and has no interest or value to you, you are not going to work very hard at it. Your motivation would be low. If you were asked to read the same chapter and then work in groups to produce a video about the content of the chapter, the task may begin to look a lot more attractive. Your motivation would probably increase.

If a student is academically confident in general, his expectation for success on academic tasks might stay high regardless of the subject matter. With this constant view of confidence, how much he values the task will guide the amount of effort he puts into it. If a student consistently expects to fail (called "failure acceptors" in the trade), you must create a learning situation in which the student *can* function. If you don't, regardless of how cool the activity is, this student will eventually give up once he realizes that he doesn't have the necessary skills to succeed at it.

Expectancy and value continuously interact with each other. A student's confidence changes regularly. Let me give you an example. In 2001, I planned to participate in the California AIDS Ride. I would ride a bike all over California. It was going to be 650 miles of grueling pleasure with a glowing sense of purpose. I trained like crazy. My overall motivation was enormously high. I expected to ride strongly and finish the ride without ever having to walk because, as I said, I really trained hard. I have friends who have struggled with AIDS so the value of the ride was off the charts for me. Once I started the ride, my expectation for success began to change. The value of the ride remained constant. But, for a period of time, I had to ride on Highway 101. Cars buzzed by me at 75 miles per hour, nearly reducing me to the status of a very large bug on their windshields. My nerves really kicked up and my fear escalated. My expectancy dropped a lot, but fortunately, not enough to pull over. I did finish the ride, but not nearly the way I had predicted because my expectancy changed during the task. The levels of expectancy and value predict the level of challenge you and your students will attempt. They predict the amount of effort you invest and the degree to which you persist when obstacles present themselves.

If there is a task that you know you can't possibly succeed at, your motivation will be zero (Tollefson, 2000). If I asked you to lift a Buick over your head, you know you can't do it so you won't even try. If I ask you to do a task that has no possible attraction to you, your motivation will also be zero. If I said, "Eat a handful of dirt," you could do it, but you wouldn't even try because it has absolutely no value to you. As each of the factors increase, the amount of motivation becomes higher. Of course, the trick is remembering to select tasks that the kids value, not tasks that you, and you alone, value. Throughout this section, we continue to amplify this theory. We begin with a closer examination of expectancy.

Digging a Little Deeper Into Expectancy

How successful a student thinks she is going to be depends on a number of things. Here are a few of the more important ones for you to consider. Think about a few of the students you have who don't try because they have a poor record of success. You will find the reasons for their thinking in the next few paragraphs.

Self-Efficacy

My first car had a stick shift. My parents and I went out to buy it before I knew how to drive a stick shift transmission. My parents drove home and the car dealer gave me a quick, superficial shifting "lesson" and sent me on my way. My drive home took three hours even though my watch said it was only 15 minutes. They were the longest 15 minutes of my life. At one intersection, I got stuck at a red light, on a hill that was at a good 30-degree incline. I had a small panic attack waiting for the light to change, and I made a fool out of myself chugging back-and-forth trying to let the clutch out. I didn't make it until the third light. To make things worse, since it was a convertible, lots of people could see that my red face matched the light I missed while I was stuck there. I finally made it through the intersection with people honking and laughing at me. After a few days of practice, I had no trouble whirring through the gears. Although it's better known as confidence, we are describing the concept of *self-efficacy* developed by psychologist Albert Bandura (1997). It's a confidence measure that's related to an individual's assessment of his skill and whether he believes he can apply those skills to particular situations. Every activity you perform has self-efficacy tied to it.

Self-efficacy has little to do with *reality* and everything to do with *belief.* Before you try something, you assess whether you think you can succeed. Your actual ability is irrelevant because your decision to act is based on whether you *think* you can do it. If you are a great basketball player, but you don't have the belief that you are, you won't try out for the team. The sad part is that you miss out on the whole basketball experience because you're not confident enough. If Margaret would be thrilled to go to the dance with you, but you believe she will turn you down, you won't ever ask her. You'll miss going to the dance with her. If your English teacher gives you a book she knows you'll love, but you don't think you can really understand it, you will never know how good it was.

As teachers, one of our major tasks is to change kids' sense of self-efficacy. If we can help them to become more confident in their academic abilities, their skills will grow as their behavior problems decrease. The problem we face is that after a student has been beaten down enough times, he gives up hope. His academic self-esteem plummets and he becomes very reluctant to stick his neck out again so that he can get additional confirmation that he's not very smart, at least in school. The more we understand about self-efficacy, the more we can help our students. Here are a few of the factors that control self-efficacy and can be useful in instilling confidence in your students.

The Nike Rule

Nike's motto is, "Just do it." By simply doing something, you learn how skilled you are. These assessments determine what you will do and how you feel about doing it. More important, these assessments are not static. They are ongoing and change faster than the weather. I was driving in traffic listening to sports radio and relaxing on my way to an appointment. Out of nowhere, the car to my left swerved into me, driving me into the car to my right. We all pulled over and exchanged information. When I got back into my car, which was still drivable, I turned the radio off and stayed in the right lane for quite a while. I nervously kept looking left and right for swerving cars. My confidence was shattered. After driving for a while, I came to realize that every car wasn't going to hit me. At that point, I turned the radio back on and drove comfortably, although a bit more cautiously, to the car repair shop. The important thing here is the progression I went through. After the accident, my self-efficacy dropped. It increased again after I began driving and regained my confidence. This is a thumbnail presentation of the Nike Rule and shows how rapidly confidence can be affected. In our classes, students have many opportunities to succeed and fail daily. How you deal with these events affects your students' decisions of whether to try again.

Modeling

Sometimes your confidence improves by watching someone else and saying, "Hey, I can do that!" When I see an Olympic diver do three flips off the high board, I tell myself I could *never* do that. But, when I see someone create a newsletter on the computer with her students, I think, "Hey, I can do *that!*" The Nike Rule tells us what we can do by assessing our own results; modeling tells us by comparing ourselves to others. Modeling lets us demonstrate how to perform tasks for our students. When you are clear and focused, students will understand what to do and get a sense of confidence just from observing you doing it (Keyser & Barling, 1981). You show what is possible for them. However, here's a little caution. Never begin a task by saying, "This is easy." It may be easy for you, but remember that your students are just learning the skill and if it is "easy" and they can't do it, their self-efficacy will plummet. You don't want them to think that if it's easy for you, it must be hard for them because they aren't smart. If you do want that, get out of teaching and go into politics.

Social Persuasion

Social persuasion refers to others telling you that you can do something. It can influence how likely a student is to try something new. At the age of 14, I went skiing with a group of my friends. There we were, at the top of Mammoth Mountain in the Sierra Nevada. There was a lot of snow and we edged out to a small cliff that looked enormous. I hadn't done this kind of a jump before and was very nervous; we all were. I knew that if I fell, I was going to slide a long way, get hurt, and as a bonus, I would look like an idiot in front of my friends. Among 14-year-olds, it is very important to avoid looking like an idiot. As we all stood there, I don't know how they got organized so quickly, but all of a sudden they all started yelling at once for me to go first. "Go for it!" "You can do it!" I wilted under their pressure. As I dug my poles in, I realized nobody in my group had ever done a jump like this. I was in the process of getting suckered into going first by my peers. But, I was 14. It really didn't matter, and off I went. It felt like I was dropping forever, but fortunately, I landed well enough to be around long enough to write this book. Never underestimate the power of adolescent peer pressure.

As a teacher, you are often the provider of social persuasion for you students. Throughout this book, we give you strategies for doing this effectively. Too much or too little is not very effective, but if you can figure out just the right levels, magic can happen.

The Power of Emotions

Psychologists used to argue whether emotions caused thoughts or thoughts caused emotions; then they realized that it works both ways. If you think about raising your hand to ask a question and the thought worries you, then you don't do it. A thought caused your emotions. If you just got a tremendous jolt of adrenalin from skiing down the hill, so you do it again, the emotion changed your thinking. Emotions work as both a driving force for your actions and feedback for actions you have taken. They have a tremendous effect on your sense of self-efficacy. Going all the way back to Aristotle's view of motivation, he believed that people seek pleasurable things and avoid things that are painful, just like adolescent students.

Self-efficacy is widely thought to be the most powerful predictor for both motivation and student achievement in all of learning and motivation theory. If you learn how to gauge the confidence of your students, and you give them challenges they can handle, you are building lifelong learners. Think about anything you've done lately. Before you did it, you examined your confidence level and interest prior to doing it. If it was a simple, pleasant task, you did it automatically and probably weren't aware of doing it. If it was a more challenging task, you gave it quite a bit of thought. Adolescent students are no different.

Attributions

I was a communications major as an undergraduate at the University of Southern California. When I was a sophomore, I took an incredibly difficult exam on communication theories. I admit that I didn't study as hard as I should have. When I got my midsemester grades, I wasn't really surprised at the fact that I had a C- in the course at the time. I went home for the weekend and talked to my dad. He asked me how I was doing and I told him about my heavy course load. I forgot to mention my frequent early morning surfing sessions. I think I may also have forgotten to tell him about my late afternoon surfing sessions too. I did tell him how I was doing academically and socially. He asked me a simple question: "Why aren't your grades better?"

I told him that the lecture hall for my communication class had over 200 people in it, and the instructor wasn't very good. He talked in circles, didn't follow the outline of the chapter in the text, and his tests were incredibly hard and unfair. Then I explained that my other course instructors were just as unfair. My father said, "With you, it's always the teacher's fault. Ever since you were in junior high school, every class you struggled in, it was never your fault. When will you own up and take responsibility for your own poor study habits?" I left in a huff. I was really angry with him for saying that. Why didn't he ever take my side? I thought my dad was a horribly unsupportive person. So, I went to my sweet mom. She was more caring and a much more sensitive listener. When I finished my sad tale of professorial injustice, she said the same thing my dad did. I was very frustrated with both of them. They just didn't understand today's college environment. It took me a while until I realized there might have been a pattern I wasn't seeing. What my father tried to do, although he wasn't as skilled as you are about to become, was to work on my attributional patterns (Weiner, 1979, 1986, 2000; Weiner & Graham, 1989).

Every time something happens to us, we try to understand why we got the outcome we did. We naturally want to make sense of our environment so we either place credit or blame on someone or something for the results. Figure 5.1 describes how we attribute our performance.

If you are internally motivated, you believe that your effort determines your outcome or success. If you are externally motivated, you believe that the difficulty of the task controls the outcome and success is a matter of luck.

The hardest part of teaching is working with students who don't have the skills to perform adequately in class. Unfortunately, there is no shortage of adolescent students who are not academically prepared to enter middle school and function at grade level. When I began teaching, I naively used social persuasion techniques to try raising their confidence. I would say things like, "Try harder and you will get an A." This is fine for students who have the ability and achievement level but are not trying very hard. It borders on the criminal to say it to kids who have no possible chance of getting an A because they lack ability or are way too behind in class. Now, I get angry when I hear a teacher tell a student who can't complete a task independently to try harder. These students don't need more encouragement; they need better instruction.

When I was in graduate school, one of my professors said that anyone who teaches underperforming students and tells them just to try harder should be incarcerated. I had a big problem with that. I raised my hand. I said, "I teach middle school. I think that a large part of my job is to get the kids engaged. To do that, I have to tell them that they can do it. It's essential to give them encouragement and support. I view one of my central teaching roles as motivator." I rarely argued with my professors, but this time I was so sure I was right.

Richard Clark is an international expert in motivation. He was the professor I was arguing with. He said, "Jeff, stand up for a minute." I was a little nervous as I stood up. He asked, "How tall are you?"

"I'm about six six" I said.

Figure 5.1 Locus-by-Stability Classification Scheme for Attributions

Locus

	Internal	*External*
Stable	Ability	Task Difficulty
Unstable	Effort	Luck

(Stability on vertical axis)

INTERNAL CAUSES CHART

	Internal Causes	External Causes
	Skill	*Components of Task*
Is the cause of this behavior stable over time?	Can the student do the task?	Reasons might include • The teacher • A difficult test • Students who were not told what was on the test
	Will	*Randomness*
Is the cause of this behavior unstable over time?	Are you trying and applying appropriate learning strategies?	The result happened for no particular reason.

Adapted from Weiner (1979, 1986, 2000).

"Let me ask you something. Let's say I took you out of school for a year or two. I provided you with housing on the beach and a personal chef. I got you on a training regimen and got you in peak physical condition. If I did all that, could you play for the Lakers?" His question just hung out there. I felt like an old Looney Tunes cartoon character who turns into a donkey with a glowing red face. He was pointing out that physical ability and cognitive ability don't matter if the goals are set *too high*. There was no way I could ever play for the Lakers.

As I thought about it, I realized that if one of my students were reading at a first-grade level, I couldn't expect him to perform well with a sixth-grade level textbook. When I told him to try harder, I would either give him false hope, which was cruel, or prove to him that I had no understanding of what he was really experiencing in my class. That would show that I was out of touch with his reality. Either way, it did not provide a good basis for a trusting future relationship. If he was performing at the first-grade level, he needed different instruction with a great deal of scaffolding, along with *reasonable* encouragement. My professor was right. Of course, I couldn't leave it at that. This happened in 1995. Since I hate being upstaged, I finally said, "You're right, Dr. Clark. I wouldn't make the Lakers, but I have a good feeling I could start for the Clippers."

Digging a Little Deeper Into Value

We have looked at a few of the things that determine expectancy, those things that determine our chances of succeeding at a task. The other side of the Expectancy-Value theory deals with the *rewards* of success. How much do we care about succeeding? We get motivated to acquire or achieve something. When the goals you set for yourself come from inside, they are things you want. This is referred to as *intrinsic motivation.*

Intrinsic Motivation

There are a lot of things I do because I love them. The rewards I get are in the form of increased feelings of satisfaction. That's the only reason I do them. I love to coach my children's sports teams. I love tennis and golf. I don't get any monetary payoff or fame from any of these activities, even though there are a few people who do. To me, these activities are intrinsically motivating because I *engage in them for my own personal enjoyment and satisfaction* (Deci & Ryan, 2002). There are certain things we see students do when they are intrinsically motivated in school. They behave differently. Some of these differences include the following:

- Choosing more challenging tasks
- Applying a greater variety of learning strategies
- Seeking feedback from people in authoritative roles
- Engaging in work without fear of failure
- Persisting through challenges at higher rates and for longer periods of time
- Helping peers excel rather than sabotaging them
- Focusing on the quality of a product rather than merely its completion

TARGET: *Increasing the Value of Educational Tasks*

Teachers who establish a trusting environment that can promote the aforementioned behaviors are more likely to develop intrinsically motivated students. Carol Ames (1990, 1992), a well-known educational psychologist, introduced *TARGET*, an acronym for a method to increase the intrinsic motivation of students in the classroom. Following is a brief summary of her system:

Task: Any task that you ask students to complete must be within their range of ability. It must be interesting or relevant to them. They must have all the necessary tools to adequately complete the work.

Authority: Students must believe that they have a sense of ownership and authority in their classroom. If students believe that only you run the show and they are expected to blindly follow, they are less likely to develop ownership and enjoyment of the work they do in class. There are many ways to involve students in more democratic classroom decision making that might be as simple as having them help you generate classroom rules and consequences. You might engage them more deeply from helping select the topics of study to having them collaborate in evaluating the project rubrics you will use before beginning a project.

Recognition: I taught at a large urban middle school. I had a core group of teacher friends who were all wonderful teachers. We all discussed curriculum and books and brainstormed ways to reach our students. The sixth-, seventh,- and eighth-grade language arts teachers regularly got together and had dialogs about selecting books that would broaden students' knowledge of literature and help them develop a deeper appreciation for reading. One teacher, Jennifer Saporito, gave her year-end awards in a way that I will never forget. She deeply understood the concept of recognition. Each year, all the teachers would go to the auditorium and read off their recognition awards. Most teachers would hand out awards with titles like "Best Writer," "Top Test Taker," and other boringly named awards. Ms. Saporito, who was an eighth-grade language arts teacher, took a different approach as she went up to the stage. Here is a sample of her awards announcements.

"Good morning B Track. I think you all know me. Eighth graders, I'm going to miss you after this year. We did a lot of wonderful things and you all made me laugh a lot. I have been talking to the seventh-grade teachers and am looking forward to getting you all next year. However, today is all about my eighth graders. This year, we read a lot of books. One particular book we read was *The Outsiders.* (There was loud, enthusiastic applause from the eighth-grade section.) I loved it too. Anyway, there was a character in the book named Pony Boy." She went on to detail several characteristics of Pony Boy. Then she continued: "The student who reminds me most of Pony Boy is . . . ." She went on and handed out her allotted six awards by chronicling different characters from this book and others. The amazing thing was that throughout the entire presentation, every student hung on her every word. She was also previewing the book for all the sixth- and seventh-grade students. At the end of the assembly, I got so motivated I went up to the library to check out *The Outsiders*. When I got there, the librarian informed me that all five copies had been checked out in the last 10 minutes, by my sixth graders! Adolescent students like recognition, if it's given creatively.

Grouping: Students need to work in a variety of situations. In addition to learning about history, science, and mathematics, students need to develop skills in working together in groups and pairs. By adjusting the way the students are organized, you develop the ability to monitor and control the learning environment. By thinking about how you organize the room, you would benefit by considering the term "community of learners" to foster a sense of collaborative learning. It's unnatural for kids to sit with their peers for hours at a time and not be able to communicate with them. More important, Russian psychologist Lev Vygotsky (1962) showed us that they often learn more deeply by discussing what you teach them with their peers.

Evaluation: If you were to ask me to identify the single most important feature of good teaching, I would say it is frequent evaluation. I keep reading about parents suing their children's high schools for allowing them to graduate when they still couldn't read. The sad part of reading those stories is that no one seems surprised. If these kids had been assessed on a regular basis, their academic problems would have been identified and solved long before high school. Evaluation, if it is done correctly, should guide both teachers and students.

- *Evaluation lets teachers know if their lessons are effective.* When evaluation is used well, it lets teachers see the effectiveness of their lessons. If teachers are willing to use evaluation data to reflect on their own teaching, they can determine which lessons interest students, what their students' skill levels are, how the academic skills required for their lessons match student skills, and how much effort their students are putting out.

- *Frequent evaluation keeps students from falling behind.* We know that students fall behind. The longer it takes for us to find this out, the more behind they get. As a student's cumulative lag increases, the more she is isolated from your instruction. Now, you must either find time to reteach her or watch her fall farther behind. The more you have students falling behind, the more behavior problems you will get and the more difficult it will be to plan instruction for the class.

- *Evaluation provides students with feedback about their progress.* If you've watched kids play video games, you know they are obsessed with their scores. Students like to know how they are doing. Good evaluation provides more than scores. It gives feedback on students' levels of understanding and choices of thinking strategies. Telling them *why* they are wrong is much more valuable than just telling them *that* they are wrong. Telling them *what* you liked about their work is much more valuable to them than just letting them know they got a good score. Students like recognition for their talents and achievements.

- *Evaluation identifies kids' needs, skills, interests, and learning styles.* Instead of limiting your evaluation to course content, you can also include evaluation of students' insights into their own learning methods. Here is a strategy I have found useful to accompany exams. I asked for student reflections about exams and gave them points toward their scores for their responses. Here are some of the questions I asked them to respond to:

  ○ What study strategies did you use to prepare for this test?
  ○ Did you use a study group?
  ○ Did you use the support Web site that comes with the test?
  ○ What went through your mind during the test?
  ○ Did you notice changes in your self-efficacy as the test progressed?
  ○ How would you study for this test differently next time?

By adjusting your thinking and using the test as an opportunity to learn about learning, we give the students a gift that will carry over long after they have forgotten what year Shakespeare wrote *Othello*. An ancient Chinese proverb says, "Give the man a fish, he eats for a day. Teach him to fish and he eats forever." The Chinese left out the most important part: "Evaluate his fishing and he will learn to fish faster and better."

Time: Following are a few key issues you need to be concerned with when you make decisions about allocating instructional time in your class:

- *How appropriate is the workload?* Remember that group projects take up significantly more time than independent tasks. As the teacher, you have to decide if group work, seatwork, or whole group instruction is the best way to spend your instructional time. You have to determine which will significantly increase the learning process for your students.

- *How are you pacing the instruction?* Good teaching has a flow to it. Good teachers know how and when to transition from area to area. You have to make sure that students have enough processing time to assimilate the information but not so much time that they become oversaturated with it.

- *Are you allowing enough time for students to finish a given assignment?* One of the hardest parts of teaching is estimating the amount of time it will take students to complete tasks. On one hand, you don't want them to be rushed. On the other hand, you don't want to give them too much time so they finish early and get off task. When you factor in the multiple ability levels, varying prior knowledge, motivation, and language differences that exist in every middle school classroom in the country, this challenge increases.

Extrinsic Motivation

The second type of goal setting we talked about was setting goals for your students. If you use the ideas mentioned earlier, you may increase the intrinsic motivation of some of your students some of the time. Fortunately, there is another type of motivation that is a bit easier for you to influence. When you are motivated by anything from the outside, it is called *extrinsic motivation.* While everyone likes to do some things for their own sake, there are other tasks that require a little jumpstart to begin. Whether it's money, fame, praise, or candy, there are times when an outside incentive is the reason why we do something.

As I mentioned earlier, when I went into teaching, I decided to teach at the most challenging school I could find. It was 1992. The unrest in Los Angeles was fresh in everyone's mind. I wanted to make a difference and teaching in the suburbs wasn't the reason I wanted to get into teaching. I was tired of hearing people talk about how inncr city kids were overly destructive and undereducated. The salary certainly wasn't the lure that got me into teaching. I began my teaching career at a school in the Los Angeles Unified School District that was identified as a "Ten School," which meant it was one of the 10 lowest performing elementary schools in the entire district. Working in this setting was what drove me into teaching.

To teach at this school, you were required to teach after school hours for four hours a week and you received $2,000 each semester for doing that extra work. I would have done it for free, but the financial incentive was to boost the extrinsic motivation of the teachers who worked there. Many teachers move up the salary schedule if they take additional approved academic units. Although teaching is very rewarding on its own merit, for many teachers, the incentives are also very important. Things like tenure, summer breaks, and salary increases matter.

I compared myself to many friends who took jobs in the private sector. They kept talking about quotas and bonuses as the motivation for working 60 hours a week. Most people work hard because there is a payoff at the end. Many educators consider intrinsic motivation to be "good" and extrinsic motivation to be "bad." The rationale was that having to provide incentives to complete tasks isn't the way we should encourage learning in schools. All students should be intrinsically motivated. Anything less is unacceptable. I heard a great phrase: "If you want to be perpetually angry, insist that everybody want what you want." A big part of your job is to find ways to offer your students extrinsic motivators to keep them involved. You will find an abundance of them throughout this book. Hopefully, in doing the work for these rewards, some of your students may discover their intrinsic motivation for some new academic areas of which they were unaware.

Goal Setting

There is a strong relationship between goals and motivation (Pintrich & Schunk, 2002; Stipek, 2002). Motivation provides the energy and goals provide the direction for any activity. The most important rule to follow in goal setting is to always set goals that are directly under your control. Setting a goal such as delivering a lesson that will interest students is a foolish goal. You can't control what your students will find interesting. A more reasonable version of the same goal would be to talk to successful colleagues to identify lessons that they have found to interest students. You can control that. You can also set the goal of giving your students choices of tasks they like best. That is also under your control. By setting goals that are under your control, you will always get accurate feedback about your level of progress. The more measurable your goals, the more accurately you can gauge your success.

Here is a guiding statement to help you set goals for your students. How children perceive the goal *setter* strongly influences the amount of commitment they have for meeting those goals. Just because you are the teacher doesn't mean your students will do what you tell them. If you want to be the kind of teacher that students follow, here are three traits that are essential to your success in setting goals. First, your students must see you as *competent*. They must believe that you are skilled and know your subject matter. Second, you must be *credible*. Your students must view you as trustworthy. Finally, for a teacher to set goals and expect to have them followed, you must be viewed as *caring*. You must show your students that you care about them through actions like providing reliable feedback and continuous support.

We work with a population who want to be adults and children simultaneously. They are shifting from "working to please the teacher" to "behaving for peer acceptance." Middle school teachers are forced to take students from several different elementary schools, capture their attention, and prepare them for high school in just three years. The elementary school concept has not changed much in 50 years. The high school concept has remained largely intact as well. Only these years, the middle years, have changed. We have moved from the junior high school to the middle school concept.

A Recap

Here are three aspects of motivation that will help guide you (Bandura, 1977). The first is *choice.* Before any of us begin to do anything, there's a choice involved. This gives students more motivation by giving them a sense of ownership in the task they are about to do. If your students choose to engage in something, they feel more committed and motivated. However, just choosing to do something doesn't mean they have the skills to achieve it. We all invest different amounts of *effort* into a job. Some psychologists believe our experience automatically dictates the amount of effort we commit to any task. Just investing effort isn't enough. You have to invest effort over time, especially when you are faced with real challenges. This is called *persistence.* The formula that shows the relationship between these three factors looks like this:

Motivation = Choice × Effort × Persistence

Remember learning your multiplication facts? The part I understood best was learning my 0s and 1s. If you remember that, you are well on your way to understanding how these factors interact. Each index has a value between 0 and 1. If any of the indices has a value of 0, there is no motivation at all. If all three have a value of 1, you would be totally motivated. If you had total choice (1) and total effort (1), but only 50% persistence (.5), your motivation would be at 50% (1 × 1 × .5 = .5). People don't usually put out 100% effort or 0% either, so their level of effort would be somewhere between 0 and 1. It makes sense to say I put out *some* effort. You can even estimate how much and say, "I put out 50% effort, but I didn't try as hard as I could." The same goes for the other two factors.

If you give a student a task that she believes she can complete, and it's a task that she values, the chance that she will invest effort and work increases (Tollefson, 2000). The greater your expectation for success, coupled with a strong value of the task, the more likely you will work like crazy to complete it. We discuss these three factors throughout this book. They guide each strategy we present.

Summary

The connection between information storage and the motivation to access and use this information is an essential connection to establish. In this chapter, it is clear that individuals organize and store information in particular ways and this storage, and its subsequent retrieval, is greatly aided by the instructional delivery methods you employ. Effective lesson planning is your greatest ally here.

The most important factor in making an effective learning and motivation link is in gauging the readiness of your learners. One of the more exciting challenges in teaching adolescents is determining who can do the work, who looks like they can but really can't, and who are hopelessly lost. As you develop these skills, often referred to as "withitness," and you learn how to set appropriate goals and provide constructive support for all your learners, you will find exponential growth in student motivation, student achievement, and in the satisfaction you have as a teacher. Carol Ames hits the nail on the head with her TARGET system, discussed earlier. Motivational experts and special education experts consistently refer to the need for time. Adolescents need time in all areas of their lives. They need to sleep more and play more. They need more time to fit in all their activities and time to socialize with friends, although many parents object to this.

Central to this chapter is that adolescents need time to process and engage with the information in a meaningful way. We make the point several times in this book that if you want to know something about adolescents, ask them directly. Teaching and reaching adolescents is similar to real estate in that it is all about "location, location, location." Know your students, talk to your students, and listen to your students. Doing these three things will make it significantly easier to implement the concepts found in this chapter.

The principles we discussed apply to almost everything you do with your students. They will generalize to every activity in your classroom. In Part 2 of this book, we present a series of exercises based on these principles. It is our intention to have readers try them out in their classes, but more important, we hope that the activities we propose will transfer to your creation of new ones using ours as a launching pad for your ideas.

Part 2

The Activities

6 Maintaining Your Activity Level

If motivating people was easy, we'd all be slim and well-toned, play the piano, and speak three or four additional languages. More important, psychologists would be poor because there wouldn't be much need for us. So, first of all, let me assure you that we psychologists are doing just fine, and motivating people is *not* easy. As a psychologist, I used to work with people who had lots of self-motivation problems. And, the heaviest problem was always weight control. Chances are that you may have had a few bouts with it yourself or watched a loved one do battle with it.

It was really easy to jump start people and get them energized to start a weight control plan. Then, after a few weeks of rigid adherence to a very strict routine, they'd come to a screeching stop. Almost all of them had the same story. They were doing well and then one day, something happened and they didn't follow the program, *just for that day.* But, it seemed that *one* day had ruined the program, so why continue? From that point on, they just stopped. Their first guilt-ridden response was that once they stopped following the program, they ruined everything, so it was over. They were disappointed with themselves, but they just couldn't seem to get started again. They felt bad about spoiling their fine records, but it was over!

Unfortunately, that explanation was the tip of the iceberg. As we traveled down below the water level to the thighs of the iceberg, we saw something much different. The program they were following had three huge flaws: (1) it was *hard* and took a great deal of effort to maintain; (2) it was *boring* and *predictable* once the novelty of it wore off; and (3) it was *slow.* They didn't see pounds melting off them every day. It was easy to start because it was new and they were wild with hope. They went through the first few days on momentum. At the beginning, as they dropped a pound or two, and it was still new, it all seemed kind of exciting, but then the slow, hard, and boring reality of the routine made it easy to quit. The dagger found in most motivational programs is that they are all fueled with excitement and hope when you start, and they then give way to hard work and boredom with little day-to-day rewards.

It wasn't just overweight people who showed this trend. Even smart, well-trained psychologists like us had these same problems. Jeff wasn't a very successful gym rat. He was great at getting started on exercise programs but not so great at maintaining long-term workout schedules. He'd go for a while and be on a first name basis with all the people at the front desk, but soon nobody recognized him there. He kept quitting. I was worse.

When I tried using Nautilus equipment at a gym, it started out exciting. I was taught to lift until all my muscles were exhausted. Then, I began to notice something very interesting. Every day, as I got closer to the gym, I would begin to feel more tired. There were days when I started out feeling great and by the time I was pulling into the parking lot I'd say to myself, "I feel so exhausted. I don't think I can get through a workout today. I'm just going to skip the gym, but I'll definitely work out tomorrow when I feel stronger." You know that tomorrow never came.

Variety Is the Spice of Motivation

Could these factors be the same ones that explain why many students and teachers can't seem to stay motivated? It's just hard to stick with any single program that requires a great deal of effort. That's why this book contains so many different motivational activities and strategies. Even though I didn't like lifting weights, there were plenty of people left at the gym who did. Clearly, there is no one-style-fits-all motivation plan. One of your responsibilities will be to keep monitoring your students. Look for signs that their motivation level is slowing down. As an activity begins to get predictable, difficult, or slow, it's important that you have a large repertoire of techniques and activities from which to select. Experiment with your students. Every exercise in this book can easily be linked back to a state content standard at any grade and in any content area. Is this book *just* for secondary teachers? No, but we believe middle and high school teachers are the ones who face the greatest challenges in motivating students. These activities are all designed to give your students the following:

- Academic skills
- Research skills
- Metacognitive skills
- Social skills

- Effective work habits
- A sense of responsibility for their own learning
- A sense of being part of a larger learning community
- A willingness to learn from and teach fellow students
- A better understanding of their place within society
- . . . and fun

Grouping Ideas

Picture this scene: you are famished. You are standing in front of a succulent buffet. The aromas are intoxicating and the variety of the food is breathtaking. It contains every food and drink you could possibly want. As you stand there salivating, you are informed that, even though all that food is within easy reach just inches away from you, for the next 50 minutes you can't touch any of it. *Welcome to the adolescent world of school.* Your students are *starving to socialize.* They're at that stage of development when their peers are everything to them. School is the one place where they get access to hundreds and hundreds of other kids. But, in their classes, where they spend most of their day, they aren't allowed to interact with them. They have to stare at you, their books, or the board, and if they're lucky, a boring video. Dante would have to create another level to describe the torture these students feel that they endure.

Nowhere in this book will either of us try to argue that group learning (also called cooperative or collaborative learning) is the *only* way you should teach. There is no magic pill for effective teaching. Motivating adolescent students is more of a witches' brew, a sprinkle of this and a pinch of that. There are many situations where independent learning is essential. There are also many times when group work is, or can be, appropriate. After visiting far too many classrooms, it's obvious that there is a need for more teachers to experiment with group-based learning opportunities. There are many motivational benefits.

Almost every exercise you see in this book has a part where students work individually and another where they work in groups. You always have a choice of fighting with nature or going with it. Going with it, and using it, is a lot easier.

We are social animals. It's important for all of us to interact, and there is no more important time for this than middle school. You can choose to make students work individually, expend countless calories in anguish, and punish them every time they talk, whisper, pass notes, or text-message each other, but that will take a great deal of your time. And, it will not make them want to stop. Here are a few good reasons why kids should work in groups.

The best way to learn is to teach.

Kids who quickly master your lesson and then explain it to their groupmates find that they end up learning the information better. We're sure that you have discovered that *your* learning deepens every time you have to teach something. Similarly, every time one student teaches a groupmate something, that student learns it a little better from having taught it.

It's a great way to learn.

In just as many cases, students who got lost when the teacher explained a concept end up understanding it *only* after a peer explains it. Don't take this as a harsh assessment of your teaching ability. On the contrary, if you know something really well, it's easy to skip over a few of the simpler steps in your presentation. These steps you skip over or combine can cause many students to get lost. When students explain what you just said to each other, it benefits both learners.

Kids are closer to the Zone.

Russian psychologist Lev Vygotsky identified an important learning concept called the Zone of Proximal Development. People are challenged when they are put in learning situations that are *just beyond* their current level of understanding. If placed in this zone and supported by the right classroom environment, this challenge triggers inquiry and question asking. The zone is based on the amount of prior knowledge students have and their capacity for learning. Their prior knowledge comes from their cultural knowledge and language skills as well as the information they have learned previously. If new material is too easy, it's nonchallenging. It's not in the zone. If it's too far beyond them, it's also out of the zone. But, when it falls within their Zone of Proximal Development, they are able to learn deeply and are at their peak motivation. Fellow students who sometimes understand things just a bit better can explain concepts to their groupmates better than you can because they are in the zone. They can give their peers ways to see things that you cannot.

Like a fine wine, groups need a little aging.

Once you have placed students into groups, don't expect them to be so grateful for the opportunity to be near their peers that they will be quiet and attentive. They will talk a lot. Give them the opportunity to do so, and be patient. Groups go through a feeling-out process. They have an initial honeymoon period where everyone seems to agree. Then, after a little while, individuals within the group begin to disagree and attitudes begin to form. Don't rush to the conclusion that someone in the group needs to be moved out or traded. Through these "air clearing disagreements," students often come to respect each other. It may seem risky, but sometimes you have to be patient rather than controlling.

The lesson of the little Dutch boy is an important one.

Sometimes students have gaps in their knowledge. When these gaps are plugged, learning progresses smoothly. When left unplugged, the entire dike can break and kids become overwhelmed and drown. Students are often more willing to expose a lack of knowledge to peers than to the teachers who will be grading them. Group members are safe and can often plug these knowledge gaps within their groups. These are gaps that you rarely have the time to discover much less plug.

We always prefer structure over chaos in groupwork.

The words *structure* and *chaos* have an ipsative relationship. We paid dearly in graduate school so we are going to use what we learned here, but we're giving it to you for free. An ipsative relationship refers to a relationship where as one variable goes up, the other goes down proportionately. In groupwork, the more structured an assignment, the less chaos that will occur in your class. Or, the less structured an assignment, the more chaos your class will experience. Here are a few important rules for you to follow when creating structured group activities:

- *Assign a role for each group member.* Roles like recorder/scribe, researcher, interviewer, reporter/share-out coordinator, and database coordinator will make sure that each group member knows his responsibilities. This will reduce conflicts because you will see to it that everyone's job is clearly spelled out. You can play with the names of the roles. For example, if you teach social studies, change the names of the roles to match your present unit.
- *Model each role for the class.* Don't assume that each student will know how to carry out her role. Model how students should carry out each task. It is also helpful if you can provide samples of previous projects so that students get a more concrete picture of your expectations for them within each role. If you are having them build something, it is a great idea to build a version yourself before assigning it. Nothing keeps middle school students on task more than knowing that you struggled through the assignment as well. You

will become aware of the possible difficulties they will encounter and you can use that information to scaffold the task better.

- *Have individual accountability in your evaluation scheme.* One of the biggest sources of conflict in groups is when there is a group grade assigned for all members of a group. This puts pressure on all of the group members in different ways. At this point, slower group members will be pushed out of working. The most advanced students will take over, while complaining that they are doing all of the work. They feel that they have to do all the work because their grade is important to them and they want the project to be good. Make sure that each student is evaluated based solely on his contribution. Group members should submit their work to you individually for grading purposes.

- *Create scoring rubrics for each task.* Eliminate as much ambiguity as possible. Let students know how each facet of the project will be evaluated. The rubrics will guide their work. Rubrics, when used correctly, scaffold group tasks.

- *Indicate specific requirements if you have them.* If you want specific page counts, font sizes, margins, cover pages, and so forth, be specific. If spelling and grammar count, let students know.

Anatomy of the Activities

They say you never forget your "first time." As you try each activity for the first time, please be patient and kind, both with your students and yourself. We are certain that by the time you are using an activity for the third or fourth time, you will have tailored it to make it fit your style, and it will look very different from what we have presented here. It is our hope that you personalize these activities. If you do, we would love to hear about what you did. The activities that follow have a structure that will help you implement them. Here are a few criteria that we think are essential for an activity to work with your students.

Personal Relevance

The activities must impact students directly so they can see some direct benefit in their participation. Always look for some aspect of the activity that students can reflect on that expresses why the task has meaning *for them.* Occasionally, there may be an activity that just strikes a student the right way and may have enough entertainment value to bypass personal relevance, but for the most part, it is an essential ingredient.

Engagement

Each activity must be absorbing for the student. We have constructed the exercises so that you can try a quick version of each to see if your students find them engaging enough. If the exercise works, you can immerse students more deeply with the follow-up activities. If not, you will see why we have included so many different types of activities.

Depth

We have tried to create activities that can go beyond where we have taken them. Today, with the Internet as a resource, you can delve into any topic more thoroughly. If you come up with great follow-up activities, we're hoping you'll share them with us.

Ongoing Evaluation

As you begin an activity, you must begin evaluating its effectiveness immediately. The sooner you can tell if it's working, the more effective you'll be in motivating your students. Following are a few of the indicators you'll want to check.

Nonverbal Cues

Examine students' facial expressions and body language for affective cues. Are they sitting forward, eagerly discussing facets of the activity, asking you questions? These are all cues that they are engaged. If they quickly go off task, begin laughing or talking to each other and continue to act like adolescent students, it's probably not the right task for them. Don't judge too quickly. Beware of premature evaluation. A task may look good to them at first and then quickly fizzle out. On the other hand, a task may take a while to generate interest but then gets them deeply engaged. Keep observing the students.

Direct Assessment

It's OK to *directly* ask them how they like the exercise. They will be very pleased to give you their opinions. They will also be pleased that you care enough about them to ask. Just the fact that you are concerned about their feelings regarding what you are teaching them is yet another great way to show that you care. The key here is what you do with the results. There is an old saying: "Never have a medical test done unless you will do something different based on the results." If they learn that you will act on their feedback, and you make it safe for them to give it, direct assessment can really facilitate student motivation.

Evaluation

Examine the work they are submitting. You can quickly determine if the activity is working by judging the quality of their work. When they are engaged, their work is more thoughtful, reflective, and accurate, and they may even have proofread it. The first activity can be found in Chapter 7. Read through it so that you can see how it fits into the motivational scheme we have been describing.

What follows are a series of activities that you can adopt, adapt, and become adept with. As we mentioned before, they are student tested. Not every one will work with every class. Use your judgment, skills, and intuition, but try them out, experiment with them, and keep the information you have read so far in mind as you infuse these ideas into your class.

These tasks are designed to effectively illustrate the ideas, concepts, and theories described in this book. They engage students in making active choices. The activities are adaptable and malleable, but all give students—and teachers—immense opportunities to develop. These activities are designed to whet your appetite. Collaboration at schools between teachers will generate even more meaningful and relevant activities. What follows are model exemplars of activities that have worked in multiple geographical locations with diverse students over a period of 20 years.

7 Teaching Them to Study

As we become more proficient at learning a new skill, we develop more profound knowledge about our own learning processes. Some psychologists suggest that it takes up to 90 hours to perfect a skill like playing a song on the piano or hitting a sand shot out of a trap on a golf course. As we develop these skills and build knowledge about how we perform an action, we are developing self-regulatory skills. Self-regulation theorists suggest that we can self-monitor many things such as our methods of learning, the social environment within which we learn best, and the actual control and allotment of time (Dembo & Eaton, 2000; Zimmerman, 1990). I could spend an hour in a sand trap without batting an eyelash because I find value in it. When I play golf, I often find myself there. There are, however, many essential skills our adolescents leave school without truly understanding and a few of them are included here. We suggest you apply them to yourself before trying them with your students, as the results can be quite interesting and thought provoking.

168 HOURS IN A WEEK

Time management is one of those horrible phrases that you know must have been created by an accountant. No, it must have been created by a committee of accountants. The key to time management is to avoid *wasting time*. But, what does it mean to "waste time"? If you sit in front of your television and watch a basketball game or a quiz show or even worse, a reality show, is that a waste of time? There's not really enough information here to answer that question. If you have no pressing tasks on your agenda and watching TV relaxes you, it's not a waste of time. On the contrary, people go to spas, do yoga, and listen to college lectures to relax. They even pay money to do it. Watching TV is only wasteful if you are doing it to *avoid* doing something you *have to do*. That's why it feels so good to waste time. Wasting time is like consuming forbidden fruit. For some of us, it's *life on the edge*. "I really shouldn't be doing this now; I have work to do." It felt good just to write that phrase. I bet Adam and Eve warmed up for eating the apple by wasting time in the Garden of Eden. So, time management is the opposite of wasting time. *Time management is scheduling the "have-to's" so you can get to do the "want-to's."*

Many people waste time because they don't know how much time they actually have available. Students would benefit from knowing how much time they have to work with and schedule themselves accordingly. They could watch any important TV show and engage in any activity, if they could plan for it effectively. Time management is the topic of this activity, so let's begin instead of wasting any more time.

Time to Start

There are several steps to this activity. Before you can begin managing your time, it's important to figure out how much time you really have to manage.

Step 1: Count the hours.

Have students calculate the total number of hours in a week. They will see that there are 24 hours in a day and seven days in a week. That yields a total of 168 hours in a week. If you want to take it farther, there are 10,080 minutes or 604,800 seconds in a week, but you and your students should not concern yourselves about that unless you have a few very obsessive-compulsive students. The important thing you are going to show them is that they should have plenty of time to accomplish everything they want, if they plan well.

Step 2: Identify allocated hours.

The next step is to determine how many of those hours are already committed to necessary tasks. Have them answer the following questions:

1. How many hours do you sleep on average each night? ($\times 7$) =

2. How many hours do you spend eating each day? ($\times 7$) =

3. How many hours do you wash and groom each day? (× 7) =

4. How many hours do you spend at school each day? (× 5) =

5. How many hours do you spend each day on homework? (× 5) =

6. How many hours do you spend each day on chores? (× 7) =

When your students total these and subtract that total number from 168, they will have an estimate of how much "free time" they have each week. There are usually two ways students greet this data. Some will see that they have an abundance of time. They will have a number between 25 and 45 hours that are unaccounted for. They have more than one full day each week to get done what they need to do. They act surprised and may even feel a little guilty about the excuses they have been using to explain their low productivity rates. If they fall into this category, you should immediately get them to read the section on goal setting and get them to start setting some goals to become more productive. We suggest that you send them to the "30 Before 30" activity (see Chapter 8). Have them review the list of goals they identified there and pick one of those items and start working!

Some students will be at the other extreme. Although they are fewer in number, some of your students will find that their number of free hours results in a negative number. They already have too much on their plates. Some students actually spend a great deal of time on their schoolwork, and they may also be involved with their student government. In addition, they may also be members of an afterschool club. On top of all that, they may participate in sports, play an instrument, maintain a Web site or two, take an advanced class, and donate time to a religiously affiliated charity. It made me tired writing all that, just as it makes those students tired to do all that.

Sometimes, time management means learning to prioritize your activities and determining what activities to *abandon*. The problem is that this kind of schedule didn't just appear full-blown. It got added to gradually. And, before they realized what was going on, they were just in over their heads. There is an old psychophysics joke. You put a frog in a frying pan and turn up the heat so slowly the frog never realizes that he got fried. Although it's an ugly joke, it describes how kids get themselves into these situations. They begin to feel that they can't give anything up without making a great sacrifice. We have to help these kids learn to make these hard decisions so that they can put adequate time into the most important tasks rather than do a mediocre job on everything.

Using a Simple Sample

Here is a sample set of data that is probably fairly representative so that you can see how the activity works:

1. How many hours do you sleep on average each night? 7 ($\times$ 7) = 49

2. How many hours do you spend eating each day? 3 ($\times$ 7) = 21

3. How many hours do you wash and groom each day? 1 ($\times$ 7) = 7

4. How many hours do you spend at school each day? 7 ($\times$ 5) = 35

5. How many hours do you spend each day on homework? 1 ($\times$ 5) = 5

6. How many hours do you spend each day on chores? .5 ($\times$ 7) = 2.5

Total = 119.5

This leaves a total of 48.5 hours a week or just under 7 hours a day of free time. Even if you throw in piano lessons, soccer practice, and actually practicing the piano every day, you're still going to end up with over 40 hours of free time a week, or about 6 hours a day.

Adolescents, who are actually just like people, get stuck in ruts. Maybe they are on the phone or surfing the Internet for hours and hours each day. I'm constantly stunned by the amount of time my daughter spends each day on *MySpace* and *Facebook*. Maybe students are in an afterschool sports program and then have to help care for little brothers or sisters. Some kids go home to an empty house and have no parental supervision, so they just hang out. Some kids enjoy looking for trouble. Unfortunately, many people with time management problems are unaware that their use of time causes them problems. Psychologists have discovered that you can't solve a problem if you don't identify the problem first. This leads to the next step in the activity: finding out where their time actually goes.

Step 3: Create an activity log.

Ask your students to spend a week tracking how they use their "free time." Many of them are shocked to see how much time they actually spend doing nonproductive tasks (aka wasting time). A slight variation on this task that reaps huge rewards is to ask them to *predict* how they spend that time. Then have them collect this data. Then have them compare their predictions to their actual time allotment shown in the Activity Log. It is important for students to recognize that everything they do is based on *choices* they make.

Step 4: Analyze the results and reflect on them.

Once your students have completed their Activity Logs, it's important to have them analyze where their time was actually spent. They need to determine which were good choices and which were not. Then they need to reflect on the wisdom of their choices. Does their current use of time prevent them from achieving their goals? Do they feel helpless in some of their current roles? Are some of the ways they are spending time under someone else's control? For example, doing chores is rarely a choice your students would make for themselves at home. If they are caring for siblings and have to feed them and put them to bed before they can focus on their own work, they may be tired and frustrated. Now that students have seen where their time is spent, it's time for them to become goal-directed.

Step 5: Identify goals.

This step of identifying goals can either be done before or after the previous step, but it's the central part of this activity. Once they have written their goals, they need to identify the extent to which they have been met and how much time there is available to meet them.

Step 6: Identify adjustments in scheduling to meet goals.

The final step in the activity is finding enough time to be able to do what is necessary to meet their goals. These time management skills will help them both in secondary school and college.

An effective way to get students thinking about effective time management is to have them look at short, intermediate, and longer range planning. Begin by having students map out their daily schedules. From there, they can move toward weekly planning and finally monthly planning.

STUDY SKILLS: NOTE-TAKING AND PREREADING

The first time I was called on to spar with an opponent in my karate class, I was petrified. As a kid, I never got into fights, and now, here I was as an adult, wearing a crisp white uniform, held together by a crisp white belt. I had taken three weeks of martial arts lessons, and apparently, my teacher thought that should be enough training for me to be able to fight. The guy I had to fight already had a yellow belt, and he wanted to punch and kick me—hard! I remember running a lot, throwing a few awkward kicks, and somehow surviving the experience with massive anxiety and a uniform that was no longer crisp but now moist with the sweat that comes with sparring after just three short weeks of training.

By the time I had reached the rank of blue belt, I could face sparring with only mild anxiety. I actually looked forward to sparring by the time I got my black belt. In case you don't know the symbolism of belt colors in karate, here's the story. Every one starts out with a white belt. This signifies that you are a novice and know nothing. As you learn, your belt becomes dirtier, and the amount of dirt shows how long you have been studying. By the time your belt turns black, you are a real martial artist. As you pass each promotion test, your belt color becomes darker. In this section, we deal with learning academic self-defense skills that will lead students to a similar level of confidence.

As we pointed out in the introductory chapters, having the expectation that you can succeed at a task is motivating. When your students develop this sense of self-efficacy, they begin to enjoy some of the challenges you throw their way because they believe they can succeed. In this section, we present some study skills strategies that will transfer to almost any situation in which students may find themselves. We introduce strategies for note-taking, prereading, summarizing, self-questioning, and test-taking. Your students will begin to notice that their study skills come in handy in almost any academic context.

I had a parallel experience when I began to study boxing. Although I was still a bit afraid at the beginning stages, that extreme level of terror wasn't there anymore because some of my karate training kicked in. Although I was just beginning to learn how to punch effectively, I already knew about blocking and moving away. I had a general sense of how to evade an attack. In the same way, you can help your students overcome the burdens of learning new information by teaching them study skills that they can use in almost any academic arena. This is our version of blocking and evading an attack. We begin with a noteworthy skill: taking notes.

Taking Notes

Note-taking is really part of a bigger skill: *distinguishing between important and unimportant information.* We are both constantly amazed at how poorly our own graduate students do on this task. We find ourselves having to cue them with phrases like, "This is really important," or "This looks like a great item to put on a midterm," or "If I had a yellow marker, I'd use it on this point." Note-taking skills will certainly help your students through-out their school careers, and it is obviously something that will help them throughout their work lives as well.

Scaffolding Note-Taking

There are a number of ways that we approach note-taking. In each case, we use scaffolding techniques to help students with this task.

Providing a Model of Note-Taking

Give your students a short lecture of 10–15 minutes. Before you begin, create and distribute a note-taking template for the lecture. Include key terms and a space for them to write additional notes on the template. They will listen for those key terms and write in appropriate definitions and comments. This template is a good way to guide them to listen for cues surrounding important concepts.

Identifying Verbal Cues

Cues let students know when something is important. An interesting exercise is to have students raise their hands every time the teacher uses one. When the teacher says something like, "The turning point of the war was . . ." or "The key to using auxiliary verbs is . . . ," student hands should shoot up immediately. When you start, the brightest students will raise their hands first and the others will raise theirs after a second or two of neck craning. If this is done long enough, they will begin to get it and you can switch to more subtle cues.

Identifying Repetitive Cues

Alert your students to the fact that important information is often repeated many more times than unimportant information. This is another good place to use the hand-raising technique for feedback until students seem to be able to identify repetition consistently.

Correcting Their Note-Taking

After another short lecture, ask students to submit their notes and you can give them feedback on which content they recorded well and which content they missed. You can also comment on their accuracy and depth of recording.

Giving Them Your Notes to Compare With Theirs

Give students a copy of the notes you think they should have taken to compare with the notes they took. Have them look at which content you thought was important enough to take notes about and the level of detail you went into for each of them.

Prereading

Would you like to double your reading speed in about five minutes? That's the question I asked my students last week. They all said they would, but not very surprisingly, they were dubious. They asked what would happen to their comprehension levels. I told them it would improve. They skeptically accepted the challenge. Here is how I did it. I asked them to read a passage containing two fairly long paragraphs and write down how many seconds it took. Then I asked them to do it again. A few groaned, but they did it again. The chorus of groans kept increasing, but I had them reread the same passage a total of four times. When they compared their first time to their final time, they ranged from a 40% increase to more than double their initial speed, and they admitted that their comprehension also improved. As I strutted around the front of the room, bragging that I had doubled their reading speeds while increasing their comprehension, they said that it was a phony procedure.

When I asked why they thought it wasn't an authentic procedure, they kept yelling that it was the same passage. The questions they had to answer were, why did their comprehension improve even though they were reading faster, and why did they miss so much information on their first reading while they were reading slower? As they were thinking about the answers, I asked them if they would like to always begin with a *second reading*, rather than a first one. That is the topic for this activity/skill.

Instructions for Prereading a Textbook

1. If there is a summary at the end of the chapter, read it first.

2. If there is an introduction to the chapter at the beginning, read it next.

3. Go through the chapter in order and read every heading and subhead.

4. Turn every heading into a question. Jot it down and answer it during or after reading the entire chapter.

5. Continue reading the first sentence of each paragraph.

6. When you get to the end, read the entire chapter.

Try this yourself before assigning it to your students. You will discover how much this skill facilitates your comprehension. Your first complete reading will really feel like your second. More important, you will understand the structure and organization of the chapter better than if you began with a complete reading the first time. By not getting bogged down with the details of the entire chapter, you will be getting the highlights only. Organization, as you learned earlier in this book, facilitates both learning and retention.

You may find it effective to start this activity with your students reading a passage four times. It really does lead into this activity very effectively.

STUDY SKILLS: VOCABULARY

The Social Vocabulary Experience

Traditional spelling and vocabulary tests, particularly in middle school, have an exalted place in American educational history. Personally, I can't wait until they are just that—history. In its traditional version, teachers give students approximately 20 vocabulary words with a test on Friday. The teacher reads the definition and the students have to spell that word correctly. The study strategy for this type of testing accesses only the lowest level of knowledge: rote memorization. Most students use index cards to study. They write the vocabulary word on one side and the definition on the other. After the test, they might remember the definition of the word, but they rarely know how it's used. Here is an alternative activity that will combine language arts and social skills that provides a lasting context for remembering their vocabulary words.

Structuring the Activity

This alternative vocabulary development activity is divided into three parts. First, the students *must* understand the definition and use of each assigned vocabulary word. Second, they need to develop strategies for introducing themselves to adults and interacting with them. Third, they need to keep an index card in their possession for several days without losing it. I'm sorry to report that this third part is probably going to be the biggest challenge for many students. Here are the steps for performing this activity.

Step 1: Give one index card to each student in your classroom.

This is the card that contains the students' vocabulary words. It must be signed by faculty throughout the duration of the activity.

Step 2: Select your vocabulary words for the upcoming week.

It is helpful if students understand new vocabulary words *before* teachers use them, rather than having students see them for the first time at the end of a unit. As soon as you present each new word, make sure you give the definition, or have students look it up right away and then check them for comprehension.

Step 3: Appear to "randomly" select the number of words students will get on their cards.

You must give the appearance that the number of words are selected randomly for each student. Your actual distribution of the words will be based on your assessment of each student's needs and capacity. Differentiate the task by giving kids who love, or excel, at vocabulary a few additional words. Give struggling students fewer words. The important thing is that you scaffold the task for them. They must feel comfortable approaching a faculty member, thus it is important that they understand the terms so they don't feel awkward or embarrassed.

Step 4: Draw a horizontal line adjacent to the word for faculty signatures.

After distributing these cards, give your students a period of time to complete the activity. This time period will be guided by how many words you have selected. Your students will then keep the cards in their possession, and during free time on campus, they are to approach faculty and administrators, strike up an introductory conversation with that staff member and incorporate one of their vocabulary words into the conversation. After they do this, they take the card out, ask that staff member to sign the card, and they move on. At the designated time, you collect the cards.

Step 5: Coach students on how to approach the staff.

Many middle school students do not feel comfortable approaching faculty members without a specific reason. While this is not necessarily a reason they will all embrace, it is a reason. It is important for you to explain the value of being able to walk up to adults and begin a conversation. In this activity, it is important that students don't just walk up to staff members, spew out one sentence that randomly incorporates a word, and then follow that verbal gaff with a demand for a signature. Model some opening statements. Role-play it with students, and have them practice the skills within small cooperative groups.

Additional Guidelines for This Activity

- *Make it a rule that adults on campus can only sign one word on each student's card.* There are always a few teachers who are more popular and approachable than others. They will get deluged with requests without this rule.
- *Don't overuse this activity or it loses its uniqueness and other faculty members begin to find it annoying.*
- *Inform your colleagues that a swarm of students will be approaching them.* If more than one of your faculty decides to incorporate this activity into the same week, consider putting the words on one card or talk about it with them ahead of time.
- *Don't go easy on lower ability students.* Keep this task within reason for each student. If one of them struggles with vocabulary or is exceptionally shy, try just two words, but make those words challenging. Hold them to the same standards for using their words and receiving signatures.
- *Have the assignment due on a Wednesday or Thursday.* If a student turns his or her card in early, you can give that student more for extra credit.
- *Always keep track of how many words they had and how many they completed.* Use their progress as a gauge to determine how many words to give them the next time.
- *Make the distribution of the words appear "random."* Struggling students feel better if they think it is a random distribution and they randomly get a lower number than the average.
- *Keep extra cards on hand in case students aren't comfortable with the number of words they were given.* You will find that some students want their number lowered, but others love this challenge and want more. When this assignment was done in the first few weeks with my sixth-grade class, the students were horrified. Most students only knew two adults on the staff, my coteacher and me. We talked about how to shake hands, make eye contact, and start a conversation. We modeled it and practiced it. Then, I turned them loose. Many were still frightened, but they made contacts on a big campus, learned how to approach adults, and incorporated vocabulary words into a conversation. When I bump into former students, many of them mention that they loved this particular activity.

Summary

Here's a scary but true story. I was teaching a Student Success course at Santa Monica College and decided to just have a little fun. I asked the students how many of them earned top grades in any class by simply completing the assigned worksheet loaded with closed-end questions by reading the given chapter one time. As they read, they would find the answer to the questions and copy verbatim from the text to the worksheet. I used this opening to get into the study skills unit, and lo and behold, they didn't laugh. I was right! Since then, I repeat that story every semester and get the same look. Since I teach motivation and learning, I often ask students if this is motivating and we generally reach the same conclusions each semester. It is motivating if the only motivation is extrinsic (grades). Students who are intrinsically motivated repeatedly claim that their interest in the subject dissipates.

The general rule with motivation is to offer extrinsic rewards only to students that refuse to complete the work. Closely related to this rule is the principle that increasing confidence builds motivational choice. The activities presented in this chapter are specifically designed to build confidence of all students to not only engage with content but to build self-regulatory skill. If we are to truly teach students to critically engage with the material, it is imperative that we teach them how to initially engage with the material and build accordingly.

8 Understanding Themselves Better

👍 A TYPICAL DAY

Except for a few friends, students only know one another as they are in school. Adolescents work very hard to create and maintain an image. This is consistent with our previous discussion of *impression management* (Leary, 1996). In this activity, they have the opportunity to take their class along with them on a typical day of their lives and visually document the experience.

You will be asking each student to take out a sheet of blank paper, number from 1 to 10, and then write down 10 "snapshot" moments that most accurately represent a *typical* day. The essence of this activity is *not to exaggerate.* Unless you hit a grand slam home run that wins a game every day, leave it off. If I was doing this activity, I might take a picture of the 405 Freeway at 4:55 p.m., any Starbucks, my office, my daughter's school, and my dog's dishes. These are simple events, but they are representative of *my* daily routine. They present an overall picture, pardon the pun, of a typical day in my life. The driving question in this activity is this: what comprises an average day in each student's life?

In a Nutshell

Simply put, students are asked to take 10 pictures that represent a typical day in their lives. They can choose activities in which they engage, interactions with family or friends, studying at home, hanging out, and so on. They may also select pictures of themselves engaged in any of the activities that form a *typical* representation of themselves and their lives.

Step 1: Storyboard the presentation.

The students have to storyboard 10 activities that represent their typical day. Next they must identify alternative photographic represent-ations of each event. Finally, they must select the photo idea that best represents each activity.

Step 2: Write text to accompany each photo.

Have students generate text to accompany or explain each photo.

- *Consult your State Content Standards.* Model different styles of writ-ing that may help your students settle on the style they want to use. Styles may include journalistic reporting, humor, straight expository text, or anything else you would like them to do. Provide samples of each writing style.
- *As the teacher, you must create rubrics for their writing.* This will guide your students' writing, making sure that they give you what you are looking for.

Step 3: Display the results.

The results can be presented in three different ways depending on your technology access and background.

- *Present on paper.* The easiest low tech way to present the students' work is to have them turn in a paper with the photos and their text. A slightly more adventurous way to display their work is to use display boards and set up the results as a poster session where students walk around and look at each other's work. This should only be done on a volunteer basis because some students do not want their personal information made public.
- *Electronically display the work.* Students can present their projects as PowerPoint presentations. Again, this can be done in a computer lab as an electronic poster session, or, it can be done individually and shown to the class.
- *Use more advanced media.* Students may actually create their projects on video. The most important consideration here is having access to a digital camcorder and video editing software. Many cell phones have video capabilities, but a camcorder will make this method much easier to create and edit. Both of these media-based alternatives should also be based on a volunteer basis to protect students' privacy.

Scaffolding the Assignment

Generate an example of this project using *your own life.* By immersing yourself in this assignment, you will understand the challenges and the emotions involved. Avoid using a former student's work as an example because this tends to become a model of the way to do the activity and you will end up receiving a group of *imitation "typical lives."*

Introduce the assignment by discussing what the word *typical* means. This conversation is critical to the success of the project. Students who embark on a quest to impress others often have a few slides of value, but they struggle with the rest. This project should be a bit of an eye-opener for the students. They should gain a new perspective on what their days look like.

Hold individual or small group conferences with students to discuss selective presentation. Make sure that their selections match the goal of exemplifying a typical day. Do not just assume that they will look at your example and immediately have total understanding.

BEST QUALITIES

Everybody likes to be seen at his or her best. For many of your students, their best is usually a well-kept secret, hidden from the other kids in school. If a particular student is a good figure skater, animal trainer, or cook, there is no place in school for that student to be seen in action showing off these skills. Sometimes, students' *best* is not a skill but a trait, such as being a loyal friend. These are the things that make us feel good about ourselves, but they are only known to a few close friends, unless we make our talents known, perhaps by playing the accordion at the school talent show.

Bad news travels faster than good news. Adolescent gossip flies around middle schools approaching the speed of the sound barrier. Unfortunately, good news is generally considered boring. Good traits and talents are even more boring. The result is that many students never get to be seen in the light they deserve. They are not valued to the extent they would be if this information was released, or better yet, publicized. This is the value of the current activity.

The Basic Activity

In a different version of "A Typical Day," the students are asked to take 10 pictures of themselves showing their best qualities. As far as equipment is concerned, almost every student has access to a digital camera or a cell phone that takes digital photos that can be downloaded to a computer.

Step 1: Storyboard the presentation.

The students have to identify each of their 10 best qualities. Next they must identify alternative photographic representations of each quality. Finally, they must select the photo idea to represent each one.

Step 2: Write text to accompany each photo.

They have to generate the text to go with each photo.

Step 3: Display the results.

The results can be presented in any of the three methods described earlier.

The power of insight these storyboard activities hold is limitless. One year, I decided to contact Polaroid to ask if they would donate a class set of cameras and film packs. As cameras are expensive, they sent me 5 cameras and 40 packs of film. My students went and completed this assignment after thorough storyboarding and thinking deeply about their pictures. They understood the concept of limited supply and didn't want to make mistakes. They took this process very seriously. The effort invested was astounding and I was stunned (but not very surprised) by their projects. Compared to the quality of writing they did on random essay projects, this writing was thoughtful and engaging. Amazing things can happen when you take standards to a personally relevant and meaningful level.

CLEANING UP YOUR ACT

When it comes to motivating adolescents, you naturally think of things like video games, sports, or cleaning the classroom. Did you just go back and read the previous sentence again? Although this may not sound quite right to you, I can assure you that kids really do like video games. OK, on the surface, I can see how you might not see how keeping the classroom clean would be a great motivational device, so, let's begin with a culture that does consider it motivating.

In Japanese martial arts classes, students are responsible for cleaning their *dojo* (Japanese word for a martial arts school) both before and after each class. And, this act of cleaning goes way beyond just picking up candy wrappers. They get down on their hands and knees and scrub the floors. They clean all the equipment. It's a serious cleaning. They consider it part of their training. It's looked at as a sign of respect for their teacher and their school. It's personally rewarding to the students because they believe that it makes them part of a martial arts community. It's a way of showing their commitment to their school in particular and martial arts in general. Here's a useful tip: never throw your candy wrapper on the floor of a Japanese *dojo*, unless you want to be intimately involved with a martial arts demonstration from the nearest student. More important, we see that it can be done. Cleaning a classroom can be motivating in some places, but will it work here, in your school?

If you ask most teenage American kids if they enjoy keeping their room clean, they'll look at you as if you just asked them if they enjoy listening to a three-hour history lecture. So just how rewarding can you make the task of cleaning? The key can be found in the martial arts example you just read. The martial arts students don't really like the act of cleaning itself; they like what it *represents*. They like what it says about them. Your challenge is to make the act of keeping your classroom clean *meaningful* so that doing it makes students feel good about themselves as they do it. This is a good start, and although it can push a little dirt around, it will not build mountains. Is there a way to get kids really *excited* about keeping their classroom clean?

Road to Cleanliness Paved With Good Intentions

To take them to the next level of immersion, begin by engaging your students in a discussion about the environment and the things that are threatening its future such as pollution, global warming, and toxic waste. Ask them how they feel about standing around passively, while past generations have ruined *their* environment. Middle school kids love to complain about the poor legacy left to them by adults who they can associate with their parents' generation. Now, here comes the payoff.

Ask them what they can do about it personally and whether they believe that their response can make a difference. Generally, students say that a single person can't have much effect. It's like the 60% of the people who don't vote. They believe a single vote won't make a difference. Try beginning with the principles of starting *small* and starting *locally.* Put students into small groups and have them each develop a strategy for making one "cleaning convert." The goal here is to come up with ideas to bring more people into their community and create a bigger effect. Then have them share their strategies and results with the class. You have begun creating a classroom community. At this point, you can see if this activity is something that generates enthusiasm. If it doesn't, it's time to try the next activity. But if it does, keep reading.

Taking the Next Step

Ask the groups to keep coming up with ideas for expanding their influence. Suggest the experiment of keeping their classroom clean. Then they can begin to spread the effect to other classrooms and build on this first, small success. Because people learn through observation, let them see how their class can become a model to effect change around them. Make it personal. If we see a piece of paper on the ground in the hallway, we can bend down and pick it up. Even though it's a small act, if everyone picked up just one extra piece of paper, our local environment would look a lot cleaner. Explain how that attitude can extend into larger and larger communities. Then ask students for some examples. If they come up dry, prime the pump with examples such as this: If one person buys a hybrid car or stops using a chemical that damages the environment, it helps us all. If two people do that, it doubles the effect.

Students often complain that the earth they are inheriting is already ruined. Here is where they are given the opportunity to reclaim it. As they begin to improve the school environment, it becomes easier to encourage them to go out into their community and begin changing things by talking to people. They begin with family members and close family friends. These conversations are nice, but are they academic?

Collecting Real Data

Each month, have the students tally their results. If each student "converts" two people, in a class of 35 kids, that's 70 more people who are causing change. All of a sudden the lights come on for many of the students, and they begin to see themselves as *change agents*. As you project the numbers, show that over the course of the school year, if each student averages just 10 converts, that's 350 people who are now working for the "cause." If each of those 350 people each converts just one person, that doubles the number to 700 people. This can become a very exciting concept. They get to understand the "ripple" effect of creating mass change. You, of course, are constantly monitoring the students to see if they are maintaining their level of engagement. If they are, keep reading.

Once It Starts Really Working

When you see that the kids are self-sustaining and already influencing other kids outside your class, they deserve some notoriety. Use your resources to broadcast what they are doing to improve the school. If you have a newsletter or yearbook, make sure the efforts of your class are being mentioned. If there is a school Web site, include your students' accomplishments there too. Make sure you send notices or newsletters home to the families, sharing this exciting information with them. Have your students document their *evangelizing*. Let students publicly share stories about converting relatives and friends. Engage them in strategy sessions to see who can come up with the most creative new idea to bring in more people. You can have a "Tote Board" that tracks the number of people the students have converted. If your kids have access to a digital camcorder, you can begin to do some really exciting things. (The price of digital camcorders seems to drop daily. Remember also that many cell phones can capture video as well.) Groups of students can become video-journalists documenting the change process. You can send them out to interview people they have converted. Students can also tell their own stories.

With their access to camcorders or digital cameras, students can go out to local restaurants and ask, "How did you get an 'A' rating for cleanliness?" Find local recycling centers and bring findings back. This can become a very engaging math project. It can equally be applied to social studies and the sciences as well. These kids are starting to understand that they do actually have a chance to impact what is going on around them. They can document their own triumphs. You can offer the story to local newspapers, radio, and TV stations.

One of the reasons why this activity works so well is that it follows a major rule of the psychology of persuasion. If you want to motivate people to change, the less they have to do, the more likely they will change. The psychological term for this is referred to as the principle of *minimalism* (Fogg, 2002). This cleaning technique is effective because we're not suggesting you bring in buckets and mops for the kids. You are asking for very little change. To get started, they just have to pick up a few paper wrappers and throw them away and then tell their friends about it. But, as you see, the effects can quickly become huge.

Dissent and Lack of Cooperation

It's always good to end on a low note. We have all had students who are oppositional and don't want to cooperate. Furthermore, we may have one or two students who are just messy and don't see any need to change. Of course it would be fun to punish them, but you can go a step farther. The research literature on punishment shows that the most effective way to use punishment is to pair it with an *incompatible alternative response*. Create a position or several positions for these students who are messy. Make it their job to monitor the room environment. It becomes their job to "lead" the effort to keep the room clean. Make it very worth their while to cooperate and very "unworth" their while if they don't. If you have three or four messy students, you can create multiple roles such as these: floor monitor, trash monitor, desk cleanliness supervisor, and so forth. When they succeed, praise them, notify their parents of their achievements and your appreciation of their work. Interview your students. Help them to document the change they went through to motivate other oppositional students. This puts them in a new role that is incompatible with their former roles and habits.

Rewards for You as Teacher

Even you get to win in several ways using this activity. Obviously, you get a group of motivated students whose commitment to satisfying projects will lead to deeper learning; but there's more. You will find that you get rewarded for having the reputation of being a teacher with the neatest room. If you were a school principal, and you had to constantly show guests around your school, whose class would you like to drop in on? As you become the "go to" teacher who the principal can count on for visits, you will build rapport with the administration. This will lead to many perks for you. You and your kids will get to feel pretty special about being the model classroom at your school.

There are still more perks for you. There is an abundant amount of research literature showing that engaged kids have much fewer classroom management problems. This means you get to spend more of your time teaching productively instead of dealing with classroom behavior problems. In addition, when you offer these kinds of ideas to your students and share in their excitement, they will keep viewing you as a caring, competent, and creative teacher. As we've said, the research literature clearly shows that students who perceive their teachers as caring like school more, are more connected to their tasks, and break fewer classroom rules.

30 BEFORE 30

When I was in the sixth grade, I had a teacher named Mr. Wood. I don't remember much about him, but here is what I do remember. He had a thick mustache, he wore glasses, and he let us watch the Dodgers-Yankees World Series games during class. Back then, the games were televised, but some of the games started at 1 p.m. There was only one assignment that

I remember having to complete in Mr. Wood's class, but it has stuck with me 30 years later. I don't remember exactly what he called it, but I remember it as *30 Before 30*.

There are many things that adolescent students haven't grasped. One of the more comical ones is their view of the aging process. To most students, turning 30 is not much different than retiring. To them, 30-year-olds are ready to begin walking with assistance or plopping their teeth in a clean cup of Polident. To them, turning 30 is almost unthinkable. That was exactly why Mr. Wood gave us this assignment. And, this was exactly why I made my students complete it as well. This activity shouldn't have any criteria except to think BIG. The entire objective is for students to look at what they want for themselves when they hit 30.

The Activity

You will not find many activities in this book that can be stated in one sentence. This one can. Ask your students to generate a list of 30 things they want to accomplish before their 30th birthday.

Suggestions for Implementation

It's a straightforward activity, but it does need a bit of structure. Here are the steps you should cover with your students.

Step 1: Model the activity.

You will need to model this activity for your students and prime them with some ideas of what "big" really means. We believe that true motivation is working toward goals that others believe are challenging if not impossible. As a surfer, I have always loved watching surf films where people surf 30-foot waves. Several years ago, most people would think this unrealistic, not to mention crazy. Would you like to fly on a plane that has zero gravity? It will be available soon, but at a hefty price. A short surfing trip on the Internet will reveal hundreds of success stories and examples of people thinking and living big. It is a good idea for you to throw out a few sample goals and ask students to determine if they are "big" or "small" ideas. Then get them to rate them on a 1–10 scale for "bigness." Finally, ask your students to provide a few samples of big goals just to make sure they have the idea. This kind of scaffolding exercise will help you get the results you want for this activity.

Step 2: Try everything before you present it to your students.

To get started, take out a piece of paper and start writing a list of things *you* want to accomplish. Since we don't know how old you are, we suggest you modify the title to fit your age. You might want to have 10 things to accomplish before your 50th birthday. Use your judgment, but think big. If you feel really courageous, share the list with your students. If you don't, share it with them anyway.

The most incredible thing about Mr. Wood's assignment was that when he returned our papers, I threw the assignment away like I did with most schoolwork, but, to this day, I still remember a lot of the things on the list. I wanted to surf a 20-foot wave. I wanted to step foot on all seven continents. I wanted to dunk a basketball. Well, two out of three ain't bad.

TEACHERS WITH CLASS

We want to increase students' motivation so they can grow. Sometimes, their growth comes about because you grow. This doesn't have to happen through growing pains. I had an attorney who came to see me because he was nervous about talking in court. He was bright and articulate, and he did very well in law school. What emerged very quickly during our first session was that the law that was taught in law school was different than the law that was practiced in court. His problem wasn't his ability to apply the law; it was the fact that he didn't have the delivery skills of other more successful litigators. I sent him to enroll in the Groundlings, a Los Angeles improv theater group. It solved his presentation problems, and he had fun. He was able to make his presentations more dramatic and emotional, which allowed him to win a lot more cases.

How are your delivery skills? Would it be valuable for you to enroll in a stand-up comedy class? Would an acting class or an improv comedy class provide some useful and maybe even enjoyable skills for you? If the answer is *yes,* then go do it. If the answer is *no,* then you probably could benefit from it even more.

We know that the first step in the learning chain is getting students' attention. If they don't attend to you, they can't learn from you. Maintaining their attention comes in handy as instruction progresses as well. Taking these kinds of classes will teach you how to communicate viscerally with your students to get emotional as well as cognitive responses from them.

In addition to performance-based classes, how about your teaching skills and content knowledge. There are very few of us who could not use an infusion of new ideas. Don't wait for your school's next inservice day. Can your technology skills use a bit of expansion and updating? The good news is that in most school districts, your salary will rise as you take more units.

Objectivity and Perception

When I took my first abnormal psychology course, the professor introduced us to the Thematic Apperception Test (aka TAT). He showed us one of the cards. It was a picture of a young boy staring out of a window, and there was a violin and bow on the windowsill. He asked us each to write down what we saw in the picture. I thought it was a complete waste of my time. The picture was so clear, why did we have to write a description to state what was plainly evident?

Having a flair for the obvious, I indulged my teacher and indicated that the boy was taking a break from having to practice the violin. He saw his friends outside playing baseball while he was stuck in the house having to practice. He longed to be out playing with his friends. After we finished writing down what we saw, he asked a few of the other students to read what they had written.

The first student said he saw a boy who was learning to play the violin. His father was a great violinist, and he was afraid that he would not measure up to be as good as his father. He didn't want to disappoint him.

The next student said that the boy was a very talented student who was taking a break from practicing and fantasizing about giving a violin recital while an adoring crowd cheered. By this time, I got it! People were revealing themselves rather than objectively describing what was occurring in a picture. The magic of the assignment was not in writing our descriptions but in hearing the variety of student responses. This is the basis for the current activity.

Structuring the Activity

Step 1: Select a picture.

Ask your students to select a picture and describe what they see going on in the interaction. You can use our pictures or find your own.

Step 2: Share interpretations.

Have students read their interpretations, or collect them, take their names off, and have them read one another's versions.

Step 3: Discuss viewpoints.

Use this as a springboard to discuss how the same events are viewed differently by different people in the news on a daily basis. Use it as a discussion of historical revisionism. It is also a very useful vehicle to discuss issues of diversity and multiculturalism.

If you are feeling daring, ask students to identify who they think wrote each version.

✍ LETTER TO YOURSELF IN 25 YEARS

Any good developmental psychologist will tell you that adolescent students are enormously egocentric and that they live exclusively in present time. Bad developmental psychologists will tell you the same thing but not quite as clearly. In the adolescent world, only current relationships and immediate triumphs and failures seem to affect what students do. Their interests are defined by their peers, and everything of importance seems to have a sense of immediacy.

Usually, it's difficult to jolt students out of their focus on anything but the present. They seem to lack perspective and make bad choices. They act as if they are unaware that they even have a future. They eat very badly, hardly ever exercise (unless they are jocks, in which case they overdo it), view studying as a curse, and thrive on adversarial relationships with authority. Way too many students begin smoking, drinking, and taking drugs at this age. If you were talking to a typical eighth grader and asked him to make the worst possible decisions for his future, you'd probably be too late; he's already made them, or he's in the process of making them even worse. We normally think that these are shallow shortcomings, but these preoccupations can be harnessed and used to increase motivation using the following exercise.

The purpose of this exercise is to get students to give themselves perspective about how their *present* relates to their *future*. This activity will give them the opportunity to examine their futures and to give themselves advice about the decisions they make on a daily basis and how those decisions will affect them in the future.

This activity is divided into two sections. The first one has students write a letter to themselves from 25 years in the future describing how their lives have turned out. The second section responds to that letter. Here are the steps for carrying out the first section.

Step 1: Have students write a letter from 25 years in the future.

Have your students write out a series of predictions about their life will be like 25 years from now. Students will use the list of *Life Factors* that follows to identify how each factor will appear in 25 years.

Imagining themselves 25 years in the future, students will write themselves a letter in present time describing how their lives turned out based on these predictions.

Have students create an original draft of the letter and then have each student present their letter within a group format to get feedback from the group.

This is a structured writing assignment. This writing activity gets students to begin thinking about how their current goals, actions, attitudes, and aspirations will be realized as they project forward 25 years. They will be asked to identify where they will be 25 years from now on each of the following factors using this format:

Life Factors

Students will fill in the following information:

Occupation: Identify the occupation you think you will have 25 years from now.

Education: Describe the type of education you will need for the occupation you selected. Identify the school(s) you went to and the degree(s) you needed along the way toward working in your chosen profession.

Mentors: Identify the people who guided you toward making good career and life decisions.

Mentees: Identify the people who you have helped along the way.

Job History: Identify the positions you held on the way to assuming your current (25 years from now) occupation.

Obstacles: Identify the obstacles and frustrations you had to overcome to get where you are.

Lifestyle: Given your occupation, describe each of the following areas that define your standard of living (25 years from now):

Neighborhood: Identify the neighborhood where you live. Identify what kinds of people live there based on their income and occupations.

House: Describe the kind of house you live in. Identify the style of the house, how much land you have, and so on.

Family: What kind of family do you have? Are you married? Do you have children? If so, how many?

Friends: Describe the kind of people you commonly associate with professionally and socially. What sorts of activities do you take part in?

Cars: What kind of car(s) do you and your family, if you have one, drive?

Luxury Items: Describe the sort of luxury items you have, including the areas that follow:

Jewelry and Clothes: Jewelry and clothes often describe lifestyles. Describe how you dress.

Media: What kinds of media do you use? Describe your TV, music systems, cell phones, MP3 players, and so on.

Technology: What type of computer setup do you have?

This is the ideal time to assess whether this activity is working with your students. Within their groups, they can assess the feasibility of their plans. They will also share ideas with one another that can be used as inspiration for a second draft of the letter. Adolescent students are very strongly influenced by the ideas and opinions of their peers. If the activity seems to be working, go on to Step 2.

Step 2: Have students answer the letter from the future.

Now that each student has written the letter from the future (25 years from now) back to the present, have them answer the letter they received from themselves in the future. In the response, each student will address the following issues:

- How accurate do you believe your predictions are? Determine if the content of your letter can and will be achieved, or is the letter simply a wish-fulfillment fantasy?
- Is this future letter a fantasy or is it a roadmap? If you believe that your letter is accurate, do your answers help you create a plan for achieving your future goals?
- What steps are you going to take now to make sure this future will happen? Form an action plan that you can follow over the next few years to help bring about the future you want.

Step 3: Introduce follow-up activities.

Students can now begin doing research on the Internet to identify the answers to the following questions:

- What institutions offer training for the field they want to go into?
- What are the requirements for admission to those institutions?
- How costly are the programs?
- Are internships available in that field?
- Are there alternative paths to the fields they want to enter (e.g., If a student wants to become a theatrical agent or a fire fighter or an interior decorator)?
- What are some related fields that may also be of interest?

Summary

What you just read, and hopefully did, are learning tasks that are intended to be valuable to the learner and relevant to the curriculum, teacher, and students. When you examine these activities through the expectancy–value lens, it is challenging to think of how any of these will result in low expectations for success. This is because we ask students to reflect on processes that affect them and influence their lives. The best teachers find ways to make the curriculum accessible. They identify the expectations for success for their students and meet them at a place where individual growth can be fostered. In addition to expectations for success and the value learners place on tasks is the possibility that what the learner is engaging with will have career and life implications.

I have a cousin who is in the seventh grade. She left elementary school with a dislike of math and science, primarily because they didn't do much of it in elementary school. Her sixth-grade math teacher supported her and built up her confidence in math and now she is a good math student. However, my cousin wants to be a writer and she takes English class seriously. The focus on papers and projects in English is significantly different than any other class. Does this have to do with the teacher? Absolutely. However, it is also significantly related to how this course fits into how she sees herself.

The activities in this section provide you with opportunities to tap into the future aspirations of students and by doing this, you are building the personal relevance of your curriculum for the learner. A learner-centered curriculum is very much in vogue, but this is not a trend. The technology revolution has established the learner as the player and operator of learning environments. It now falls squarely on the teacher's shoulders to motivate students by enhancing task value. Simply put, telling them to read a given chapter and complete the questions at the conclusion of the chapter just isn't going to cut it anymore.

9 Culture-Based Activities

👍 A CULTURAL EXCHANGE

Billboard Magazine created a 24-minute tape of every number one hit song for a 25-year period. Each song was on for only a few seconds, just long enough to recognize it, and then it went to the next song. I played it for a university class I was teaching and the results were mesmerizing. If you put an oscillator (a device that generates a tone at any pitch) in the middle of a room and played a continuous tone that increased in one-cycle/second increments, every object in the room would vibrate when the tone hit that object's resonant frequency. That's what happened in my classroom with the Billboard tape. At some point, I saw every student resonate to one or more songs. Most students would sit there, and then all of a sudden a song snippet would come on and one or two students would smile or look sad or tap their fingers. You could see which students were hit with memories by each song. Every student went through many of these reminiscences.

Music plays a huge role in everybody's development. At no time does it play a larger role than in middle school. As you've discovered on a daily basis, middle school students are at a stage of development where they want to distinguish themselves from the generation(s) that came before theirs. They want to feel that they have unique traits and characteristics that older people don't understand. Music is one of the central elements. If you want to develop a bond with your students, there is no more intense vehicle you can use than music. Add giving the students an opportunity to teach you about their music and the results increase enormously. That is the focus of this activity.

Organizing the Activity

CAUTION: It is important to structure this activity carefully because a good deal of contemporary music content is not appropriate in school. This point must be clearly established before any other step is taken. Only songs with appropriate lyrics can be used. Once that understanding has been made clear, go through the following steps:

Step 1: Divide the class into groups.

This is one group activity where any kind of group organization can work. You can have students self-select their groups, or you can assign students heterogeneously, by ability—any organization you want to use will do.

Step 2: Assign roles within each group.

Each group member will have a unique role. For example, in a group of four, each student can be responsible for analyzing one of the following areas:

- **Lyrics**: a great deal of today's music is a form of urban poetry. Analyzing lyrics as poetry is a natural segue for studying other poets and great writers. Looking at the content, rhythm, and flow of lyrics will transfer easily to other forms of literature.
- **Music** (sound, melody, beat, rhythm): analyzing the music and comparing it to other musical forms and historically based music will give students a bridge to appreciating other forms of music and identifying the roots of the music they may not have discovered before.
- **Artist** (background, musical influences, etc.): presenting a history of the artist can tie in many aspects of diversity, multiculturalism, and art.
- **Genre** (this ties to the California state standards in language arts): identifying the genre to which a piece of music belongs opens the door to comparing it to other genres. It is a good way to learn about the historical, cultural, and musicological elements of students' favorite songs.

Step 3: Have students scaffold the lesson.

Show students how to explain their topic. Explain how to differentiate each group member's aspect of the song. Suggest using parts of their song contrasted with other artists, or the same artist with a different song, or even a different genre to show similarities, differences, and historical ties.

Step 4: Give the final presentation with one of your own favorite songs.

It is important that you listen carefully, show interest, and ask questions about their music to demonstrate your belief in the significance of it. You must also make sure that you get the same respect from the students when you demonstrate your song preference.

The study of anthropology shows that there is a set of cultural universals, things common to all cultures. For example, sharing food is a way that all groups honor guests and show a sense of welcome. Music is also a cultural universal. A study of any culture isn't complete without looking at the type of music a group played and listened to, and the cultural functions it had within its traditions.

HISTORICAL NEWSPAPER

Did you read the paper this morning? If you did, in a few minutes you found out the top stories of the day, how your investments were doing, what new movies were coming out, how your sports teams were doing, and tons of other information that was there if you were interested. You also could have seen what jobs were available, the price of new or used cars, art openings, reviews of new books or plays—the list goes on and on. If you really wanted to know what was going on in the 1920s, to get a real feel for what life was like then, you could go to a library and look at a daily paper from that time. It would give you a very accurate snapshot of what life was really like. In this activity, you will give your students a chance to create a newspaper for a specific time in history. The entire class will work as the newspaper staff to put out one edition of the paper. It is a powerful way to build a learning community within your classroom.

Structuring the Activity

A newspaper is made up of many different sections. You will be dividing up your students into groups that represent each one. In doing this, your classes will get a very deep understanding of a historical period and culture. They will not limit their knowledge to a series of names and dates but immerse themselves deeply into historical events as well as day-to-day lifestyles. Here are the steps for creating the activity.

Step 1: Select the historical time and location for the newspaper.

Initially, you should consult your state standards to see what choices you have within those standards. Then consult with your students in making the choice. In some cases, they may not have enough prior knowledge and you will have to supply some information so that they can make an informed choice.

Step 2: Identify the sections of the newspaper and explain each of their functions.

Begin with the following list:

- **News**: This section will be presenting the straight historical narrative of the time period. You should have your students select a day when there was a significant historical event.
- **Editorials:** This section discusses opposing sides of controversial issues of that time. This is where you can teach critical thinking skills. It's also a good place to discuss historical revisionism. You can show them how history has been rewritten to suit certain people's needs.
- **Business:** This section shows how the economy worked. It shows the products that were being manufactured, the agriculture system, investment opportunities, and so forth.
- **Science and Technology**: This section shows what was happening in the fields of science and math. It shows who the leading inventors and scientists were and what they were creating and discovering.
- **The Arts:** In this section, students can discuss the famous artists of the day and include samples of their works. They can also present reviews of current music. The review would actually be a description of the type of music of the day.
- **Book Reviews:** The book reviews tie in literature that was current at that time.
- **Advertising:** The ads in the newspaper show how people dressed, what tools they used, what they ate, and so forth. The ads are the window to the day-to-day activities of the people living there.
- **Want Ads:** The jobs that are listed here give insight into the type of work people were doing at that time.

If your school is structured for it, assemble a group of teachers from different disciplines and ask them to take part in this project. If not, ask some of your colleagues in various disciplines if they would serve as "guest experts and advisors" for your students. If they do, make sure your students acknowledge them in the newspaper.

Summary

This activity embraces the collaborative nature of motivation. Group level motivation and collaborative learning opportunities offer many unique components and tremendous learning opportunities for both teacher and student. Students learn accountability and responsibility to groups. They learn about social loafing and how to deal with it. These activities enable you to facilitate learning experiences through both cooperation and collaboration. There are few work environments today that don't expect employees to know how to work in groups and with teams. This is a skill that is not necessarily taught at any one particular level of school. It may dangerously fall into the category of education best described as this: "That isn't my area/level; I thought they should have had it before they got to (insert your grade level)." Fundamentally, adolescents need many opportunities to engage with each other in structured environments with high expectations for success and production. They also need support through this process. These activities build on all components of learning and motivation by analyzing strengths and weaknesses of groups and individuals within the groups as well as developing presentation skills. They are rich in relevance as you enable students to select areas in which they are most comfortable.

The next section introduces you to the role of technology in learning. As you read, exercise caution with the belief that the mere presence of a computer decreases motivation. Technology is simply a tool to learning, not the answer to all educational solutions. As with any tool, it is critical that users have a clear understanding how to use it, when to use it, and why they are using it.

10 The Technology Mismatch

Introduction

At the end of a typical school day, my 17-year-old daughter comes home, turns on her TV, turns on her computer, and picks up the phone to call a friend. Then she selects the program she wants to watch, takes out her homework, goes to her MySpace or Facebook to see which friends have contacted her, and then she begins IMing (i.e., instant messaging) several friends, one after another until she's chatting with at least four or five of them. Any two of these tasks done simultaneously would unnerve most of us, but for my daughter, and millions of adolescents like her, it's just "another day at the (home) office." This is the way she operates. She grew up "digital." She has never known a time before computers, e-mail, the Internet, and cell phones. Texting is her favorite mode of writing; e-mail is old-fashioned and not immediate enough for her.

My daughter can multitask incredibly well. Is there a price she pays for being able to split her attention like this? Unfortunately, there is a price and it is quite high. When she has to read a schoolbook or listen to one of her teachers lecture at school, she has a serious problem. The pace is way too slow for her. She has trouble paying attention. She does not have ADD (i.e., attention deficit disorder); she is *typical*. When I try to have a conversation with her, she fidgets and squirms, unless it's a topic she likes or a topic she chooses. The key word here is *choice*.

Many adolescents today function really well *if* they can control their own learning environment. They function well in an interactive world. If they watch TV, they clutch the remote control and use it a lot. When they are looking for information on the Internet, they search very rapidly, flying from link to link with incredible speed. I get a headache watching my daughter finding the information she wants. Adolescents can tell in an instant if there is something of interest for them there; if not—adios! They like to choose. Now, they walk into your class on a day when you're going to tell them about the *Monitor* versus the *Merrimac* or the Treaty of Versailles. Good luck keeping their attention!

The Problem

We have a real serious problem on our hands in *two* directions.

1. *Teachers must learn to deliver information in ways that are congruent with the ways students prefer to get their information.* Donald Leu made an interesting point in his 2005 presidential address at the National Reading Conference. There are no schools in the United States that let students use a word processor on state writing proficiency exams. A study showed that 19% more Massachusetts students passed the state writing tests when using word processors than writing by hand when they had the choice.

2. *On the other hand, students must learn to adapt to more traditional classroom methods because they will encounter those methods throughout their education and when they enter the workforce.* There are unique challenges for each group.

New Learning for Teachers

Teachers must learn to present information in a way that is closer to the way students like to obtain information. Teachers must adapt their information delivery skills to accommodate a style more compatible with their students' style. There is an age gap in technology. I was talking to a 20-year-old student and mentioned that I had texted a message to my daughter and he looked at me with wonder in his eyes and said, "You text?" It was not meant as a compliment. He didn't think people my age knew about texting, much less did it. Teachers must learn more about the new technologies their students use for hours every day.

New Learning for Students

As important as it is for teachers to move closer to using the methods students use to get their information, students must learn to function better in the more traditional educational settings where books are read and teachers are listened to. Students have to learn to read books that are written in a linear structure with a single narrative voice. They must be able to focus their attention without hypertext. Harder still, they must be able to sustain their attention when listening to you talk about a topic they did not choose. The activities in this chapter will help both students and teachers move toward the center.

A New Instructional Paradigm

As teachers, we must learn to shift from looking at our students as *learners* and begin to see them as *information managers.* There is no reason why a teacher should ever teach students the capital of Kansas. Why? This is because they will forget it very quickly if they don't *need* to know it. If they just memorize it for a test, it is boring and a waste of time. We should be more concerned with teaching them how to find information and what to do with it once they find it rather than focusing on what information we think they need to retain.

More than half of the information I learned in graduate school is now obsolete or just wrong. I would be worthless as a scholar today if I hadn't learned how to keep current and find new information. We begin with the students. Getting them to sit through a lecture containing information they want is difficult, and when it contains information they don't want, it's often a nightmare.

GETTING STUDENTS TO LISTEN WHEN YOU TALK (INCREASING THE INTEREST SPAN)

These digital students have a very short attention span for uninteresting information. *Interest span* would probably be a better term than attention span. As teachers, there are times when we want to expose our students to some valuable information and it is most convenient to use the lecture method. Here is a way to help your students increase their interest span when listening to you.

Step 1: Have students give short classroom presentations.

Assign topics that they research and then report on. When you first begin doing this, keep the presentations short, lasting no more than five minutes. Students do better paying attention to short presentations, especially from their peers. They empathize with their classmates and tend to be very supportive because they understand the terror of facing a class themselves. This is especially true when they've just done it and even more so when they are about to do it.

Step 2: Create evaluation rubrics for students to do peer ratings.

Peer evaluation increases students' motivation. The presentations become more interactive. A dividend for you is that it gets your students to understand what goes into a presentation so that they won't take your lectures for granted. In addition, of course, it will help them learn the valuable skill of presenting. Make the evaluations both written and anonymous. Have students receive their scores and feedback *without* you seeing it. When feedback is anonymous, students can give each other more honest feedback without worrying about their evaluations affecting their peers' grades.

Step 3: After your students have given their presentations, begin to give some short presentations yourself.

Keep your presentations under 15 minutes in length. After each presentation, have your students evaluate your presentation using the same rubrics they just used to evaluate each other. This will add a new dimension of interest to your presentations and make them more interactive because the students are no longer passively sitting and listening. They are now cast in the role of evaluators. A bonus for you is the feedback that they will give you. Read that feedback carefully, and if it is useful, use it! You can also discuss the feedback with them. Hopefully, after they have tried presenting and then watch you, they will appreciate your efforts more.

Step 4: Introduce interactivity into your lectures by using Quick-Thinks.

You learned about Quick-Thinks as part of scaffolding in Chapter 4. Adding Quick-Thinks every 10 to 15 minutes gets your students involved. To use Quick-Thinks, stop your lecture every 10 to 15 minutes and put your students into pairs or small groups. Have them discuss questions based on your presentation. The more actively they participate, the more interest you will generate and the more they will learn. Remember that elaborate rehearsal produces the best understanding retention.

At this point we turn to things that teachers can do to become more familiar with the way students like to learn. We begin with WebQuests. We selected this topic because it follows the principle of minimalism (Fogg, 2002). The less you, as a teacher, have to change, the easier it is to motivate you to change. You can begin using WebQuests immediately, even if you have never touched a computer before. They are self-contained. You only have to present them to your students and they take it from there.

USING WEBQUESTS

Although there are many ways to integrate the Internet into instruction, we have chosen WebQuests because they embody everything we believe good Internet-based instruction should contain. WebQuests were developed by Bernie Dodge (2007) at California State University at San Diego. They have been used successfully throughout the country for years. Here are just a few reasons why we selected WebQuests:

- *There are abundant resources, lessons, and examples available for free on the Internet.* As a teacher, you can begin by using already existing WebQuests with no previous training. They are all laid out and ready for your students to begin using. The following link will take you to hundreds of WebQuests that have already been evaluated and are ready for your use. They are also catalogued to correspond to state content standards: http://webquest.org/search/.
- WebQuests *embody the constructivist view of teaching.* They provide excellent examples of authentic assessment, scaffolding, project-based group instruction, critical thinking, and guided discovery learning. They are the very model of engaged, active learning. According to Bernie Dodge, the goal of a WebQuest is knowledge acquisition and integration. This is done through inquiry-oriented activities with resources on the Internet. The following link will highlight many features of WebQuests that make it an effective way to introduce both students and teachers to using the Internet for research: http://webquest.sdsu.edu/about_webquests.html.
- *One of the main features that distinguishes* WebQuests *from other Web activities is that the Internet links are already put in place by the WebQuest designer.* The focus is on using information rather than looking for it. This keeps students safe from sites that are not appropriate for adolescents.
- WebQuests *are also different from other Web-based lessons and experiences in that they focus on an engaging and achievable task.* Ideally, the task is a scaled-down version of something adults do on the job. WebQuest tasks go beyond simply answering questions; they require higher order thinking skills such as creativity, analysis, synthesis, judgment, and problem solving.

Designing WebQuests

Once you have had your students working on WebQuests, you may find that you want to begin developing you own or have your students get involved in developing them. Bernie Dodge has created a series of WebQuest templates to make it easy for teachers and students to design their own. The following link contains these templates, which provide scaffolding for every step of WebQuest creation. The best part is that it is all available for free: http://edweb.sdsu.edu/webquest/LessonTemplate.html.

Bernie Dodge has very generously placed online an entire week's curriculum for learning how to develop WebQuests from his Summer Institute at the Chadwick School. The following link will guide you through the entire process: http://edweb.sdsu.edu/webquest/webquest webquest-hs.html.

The following link will take you to a tutorial that begins teaching WebQuest design. No previous skills are necessary: http://www.teachers first.com/summer/webquest/quest-a.shtml.

Parts of a WebQuest

A well-structured WebQuest contains six elements: introduction, task, process, resources, evaluation, and conclusion. The following link takes you through each of these sections and provides examples of each: http://projects.edtech.sandi.net/staffdev/buildingblocks/p-index.htm.

The following link by Kathy Shrock provides an excellent WebQuest about using search tools on the Internet: http://www.sdst.org/shs/library/sqteach.html.

Scaffolding

Dodge emphasizes that WebQuests often contain skills that push students beyond their current limits, making it essential to provide scaffolds to support students. There are three types of scaffolds:

1. **Reception**: These are guides to learn, organize, and remember information (e.g., glossaries or observation guides).

2. **Transformation**: These structure information for a specific task or purpose (e.g., Venn diagrams or feature charts).

3. **Production**: These produce a product based on the information (e.g., outlines and templates). The following link provides clear examples of the way in which student learning can be guided by the

use of clear structuring so that learning is facilitated by context and organization: http://edweb.sdsu.edu/webquest/necc98.htm.

For more in-depth information about the use of scaffolds in WebQuests, visit the following link to see Jamie McKenzie's (1999) explanation and examples: http://www.fno.org/dec99/scaffold.html.

Evaluating WebQuests

As you and your students create your own WebQuests, you will want to know if you are maximizing the potential of this format. The following link provides a rubric for evaluating WebQuests. You will find criteria for all six areas as well as an overall aesthetic rubric: http://edweb.sdsu.edu/webquest/webquestrubric.html.

PODCASTING

Imagine your students listening to their iPods, but instead of listening to music, they're listening to you talk about history or literature or anything else you'd like them to hear. This is the bold vision we are offering in the form of the podcast. Podcasting will improve your use of technology and bring you closer to the skills of your students. Since so many of your students have iPods or other MP3 players, they will feel very at home with this activity.

Podcast Overview

A podcast is an audio or video file that you can place online for students to download into an iPod or other MP3 player (Cochrane, 2005). It is delivered through an RSS feed. RSS stands for *Really Simple Syndication*. It is a type of Web feed format used to publish information that is updated a lot. In addition to podcasts, RSS feeds are also used for blog entries and news feeds on the Internet. The biggest advantage in using podcasts is that they let your students select the time and the place they want to play back your lessons and broadcast content.

Podcast Uses

Although it may not happen in your class, teachers report that some of their students are occasionally absent. Instead of having to reteach to those students or have them fall hopelessly behind, teachers wear a lavaliere microphone whenever they teach and record everything they do. Then they make each lesson they teach into a podcast for students who missed class or for those who want a review. Some teachers use them to present extra resources. For example, a history teacher might provide samples of the music played during a particular period of history.

You can also have students create podcasts as a form of presentation or project. They can use it to create news reports and theater arts projects. Now that Podcasts can also use video, it opens up a world of possibilities, limited only by your imagination.

Podcast Creation

Step 1: Gather the tools.

To produce a simple audio podcast, you only need four things: a computer, a microphone, and a Web site, along with software that can be downloaded from the Internet. As far as a computer is concerned, if you have a computer that can run Windows XP or a Macintosh computer that can run OSX, you have enough computing power to create a podcast. Any microphone that will record sound on your computer will work. Any software you have for recording and editing will work. If you don't have any, you can download a copy of *Audacity* for free from the following site: http://audacity.sourceforge.net/.

Step 2: Upload your podcast.

To upload a podcast to your Web site, use an FTP program capable of error checking. This will make sure that the file you transfer is an exact copy of what you recorded. An FTP program moves a file on your computer to a file directory on the server where your Web site is hosted. There are hundreds of FTP client software programs available, many for free. Cochrane (2005) strongly recommends the two programs that follow.

1. **Windows** (*WS_FTP Pro*): For Windows-based computers, he recommends WS_FTP Professional. It is available at http://www.ipswitch.com/Products/WS_FTP/com/Products/WS_FTP/.

2. **Macintosh** (*Captain FTP*): For Macintosh computers, he recommends Captain FTP. It is available at http://www.captainftp.com/. *Fetch* is also a reliable program; it costs $25 and is available at http://fetchsoftworks.com.

Following are three sites that offer podcast resources you may find useful in your classes. This way, you can get all the benefits of podcasts without having to create them yourself. It is also a good way to get your introduction to podcasting.

1. **Apple Podcast on iTunes:** http://www.apple.com/itunes/store/podcasts.html.

2. **iPod U**: This is Apple's use of the iPod in education. There are tons of educational podcasts ranging from K–12 through university-level programs available for downloading at http://www.apple.com/education/itunesu_mobilelearning/itunesu.html.

3. **Podcast Directory:** http://www.podcast.net/.

DOING RESEARCH ON THE INTERNET

The final activity in this section is doing research on the Internet. It is an essential skill, actually a set of skills, that will help you and your students become lifelong learners. As you will soon see, Internet research is more involved than placing a keyword in *Google* and pressing the return key.

A Model for Acquiring New Information

Leu, Kinzer, Coiro, and Cammack (2004) lay out the differences between traditional literacy and "The New Literacy" that includes the many skills necessary to find information electronically. In the course of a typical day, today's students may encounter Web logs (blogs), word processors, video editors, Internet browsers, Web editors, e-mail, spreadsheets, presentation software, instant messaging, plug-ins for Web resources, Listservs, bulletin boards, text messages, avatars, virtual worlds, podcasts, and wikis. If you are reading this short, and very incomplete list and find that you aren't familiar with some of these terms, you can use it as an index of how much you have yet to learn.

In this section, we focus on the most crucial skill we think students must master: finding and using research information on the Internet (Desberg & Fisher, 2001). This is a comprehensive, six-stage model that goes from identifying a research question all the way to disseminating the results.

Step 1: Epistemology—Identify the question.

A student is assigned or selects a topic such as "labor unions" or "whales" or "smoking." Within a short time, the student discovers her need for epistemology; she just doesn't know it by name. Epistemology is the branch of philosophy that deals with knowledge. It is defining questions and identifying what information is needed to answer those questions. This is where students have their first major difficulty in a research project. They identify a broad area and dive into researching it. Later, when they find themselves overwhelmed, they are finally forced to begin narrowing down their topic, more often for the sake of convenience than scholarship. The operative word here is *overwhelm.*

Example

To keep this skill concrete, here's an example. If a student begins a paper on the topic of "smoking," a painful discovery is soon made that it's too broad of an area to research. A quick investigation turns up the fact that there are legal aspects, health aspects, economic aspects, political aspects, agricultural aspects, and many, many more, each with mounds of information contained within it. So, the initial discovery is that it's not enough to select "smoking" as a topic. On the way to figuring out what a research paper will be about, there are four steps students must perform:

1. Choosing a topic

2. Limiting the area

3. Focusing on the question

4. Identifying what data is necessary to answer the question

1. Choosing a Topic

Choosing a topic refers to limiting the area or scope of a project. An effective way to begin is with a brainstorming session. Have students list everything they know about a topic. The students can then select one of the areas they've listed. For example, they could choose health risks. The students can also browse encyclopedias or other reference sites and books for additional ideas. Following are a few useful Web sites that present more in-depth discussions and resources for helping students choose a topic:

http://collegeuniversity.suite101.com/article.cfm/choosing_topics_
for_term_papers

http://www.library.uiuc.edu/ugl/howdoi/topic.html

http://www.bates.edu/x25876.xml

http://www.lib.iastate.edu:9050/resources/topic/index.html

2. Limiting the Area

Often, the topic they select is too broad. A search that returns too many items results from entering keywords that are too common on the Internet. The student ends up with hundreds, thousands, or even millions of hits. To narrow down a topic, the student can begin by searching *Web directories.* These are Web sites that are cataloged by subject. As students know what they are looking for and can come up with more precise search words, they can create more productive keyword searches. Web directories will suggest ways of carving up an area to show students the way certain areas are organized.

Web directories have to be assembled by people. In contrast, pure search engines create weak subject classifications and compile their databases with Web crawling software. For this reason, Web directories are often helpful for beginning a task. For example, if you have a broad subject that you would like to narrow down to a specific topic, you can just follow the subject links in the directory down to the editors' topic and subtopic menus for inspiration. Following are a few useful directory-based search engines:

Yahoo—http://www.yahoo.com

Google Directory—http://www.google.com/dirhp

About.com—http://www.about.com/

Search.com—http://www.search.com/

Open Directory—http://www.dmoz.org/

1UpInfo—http://reference.allrefer.com/

To find out more about selecting the best search engine for your needs, use the following site. It compares information about different search engines and helps students decide which would be best for them: http://www.virtualsalt.com/search.htm.

3. Focusing on the Question

After limiting the area by narrowing down the topic, the student must focus on a specific question to answer about the selected area. For example, if the health issue is selected, the student might ask questions such as, "What are the health risks of smoking?" or "How do the tobacco companies interpret the research differently than universities?" The process is one of continuously narrowing down the topic until a single, *researchable* question is selected.

4. Identifying What Data Is Necessary to Answer the Question

The final step is the most often ignored area in teaching: helping the student decide what kind of data is necessary to answer the question and draw a conclusion. Using our example, the student must decide if only research evidence about smoking is acceptable or if expert opinion is valid as well. If expert opinion is valid, what are the criteria for someone to be considered an expert? These are critical skills that are rarely taught, and the punishment we receive for this omission is evident in areas such as advertising and politics.

Step 2: Locate information.

Students now have to locate information by using one of two types of search engines: directories and pure search engines. Directories, also called "subject catalogs," are hierarchical listings of topics arranged from broad-to-specific. Directories are assembled by people. Search engines compile machine searches through large databases using intelligent operators called *spiders* or *robots.* They look for key words in titles, text, and metatags that are written into the HTML source code of a Web page. Many search engines are actually a combination of a directory and a search engine. Following is a valuable site for comparing the benefits of search engines: http://www.searchengineshowdown.com/.

Because search engines don't rely on people to create directories, there is no lag time between when a site is posted and when it becomes available on the Internet. Because directories tend to be broad, you will find information that is often esoteric, tangential, or just irrelevant to your specific topic. Each search engine uses a different search strategy. You should become familiar with several of them because each ranks the importance of search results differently. Search engines use programs called spiders or robots. They gather new documents on the Internet and place them into a database. When you make a request, they search the full text of the document.

Each search engine works with different rules and strategies. Some are more intelligent and can discriminate which words are significant in searches. Some search engines just look at the titles of sites while other search engines search metatags. These are key words that do not appear in the document but are placed in the HTML source code for indexing.

Searching Strategies (Too Few Items Returned)

Once your students have selected their research questions, they will enter a keyword in a search engine. In a heartbeat or two, they will see how many items the search engine returned. If there are not enough items, here are a few strategies students can use:

- *They can try using some broader terms.* For example, if "emphysema among Hopi tribes" was too specific a term, they can try "emphysema among Native Americans." If that is still too specific, they can try "emphysema."
- *They can use alternative terms.* If "Native Americans" doesn't work, they can try terms such as "Indians" or "indigenous natives," or they can enter words like "tribal" or "reservation."
- *They can use a thesaurus, which is useful for generating alternative search terms.* Libraries have subject-specific thesauruses that can be even more helpful for finding useful keywords.

Searching Strategies (Too Many Items Returned)

A more common problem is when there are too many items returned in a search. In this case, the following strategies are useful:

- *The more search terms students add, the more narrow and specific their search will become.* Each new descriptor eliminates a large percentage of returns in a search. Play the "emphysema" example backwards to see what we mean.
- *Using phrases rather than single words will narrow their search results.* This is a helpful way to reduce the number of items returned.
- *Eliminating or replacing generic terms with more specific ones will narrow their search results.* Enter commonly used words that make your original description more specific.
- Using Boolean operators like the ones that follow will narrow their search results:
  - AND searches find pages that include only sites that use BOTH of the terms.
  - OR searches find pages that include EITHER of the words or BOTH.
  - NOT (e.g., science NOT fiction) searches finds pages that include the first word but not the second (e.g., pages containing science but NOT science fiction).

Step 3: Determine the credibility of sources.

Just because something is in print or said by an expert does not make it true. There is a basic law of the universe that says, "For every PhD, there is an equal and opposite PhD." Students must learn how to determine if the information they are getting is from a valid source. If a student is interested in researching the effects of tobacco on disease or addiction, would a tobacco company site be an appropriate location from which to get all of their information? How would it differ from going to the American Cancer Society Web site?

Information is rarely neutral. Information is often used to persuade. Because data is used in selective ways to form information, it generally represents a point of view. Every writer wants to prove his point and will use some form of data to do it. When evaluating information found on the Internet, it is important to examine who is providing the information you are viewing and what might be their bias. The popularity of the Internet makes it the perfect venue for commercial and sociopolitical publishing. These areas in particular are open to highly *interpretative* uses of data. Following are a few of the criteria you can use to evaluate the credibility of a site:

- **Breadth**: Are all aspects of the subject covered, or is only one point of view presented?
- **Content**: Is the information based on fact or opinion? Does the site contain original information or simply links? Sites can be useful both as information resources in themselves and as links to other information. However, users can be frustrated by lists of resources that look promising but turn out to simply contain more links.
- **Accuracy**: Is the information in the resource accurate? It's a good idea to have your students compare the site's information with other resources or check some information about which you have special knowledge. Are there political or ideological biases? The Internet has become a prime marketing and advertising tool, and it's a good idea to have students ask, "What motivation does the author have for placing this information on the Internet?" Often the answer is that the information is placed to advertise or support a particular point of view.
- **Authority**: Does the resource have a well-respected organization or expert behind it? Does the author have standing in the field? Are the sources of the information stated? Is the information verifiable? Can the author be contacted for clarification or be informed of new information?

  In your own field of study, is the author a well-known and well-regarded name you recognize? When you find an author you do not recognize, is the author mentioned in a positive fashion by another author or another person you trust as an authority? Was this site linked from another reputable site?

Does the Internet document you are reading give biographical information, including the author's position, institutional affiliation, and address? Is biographical information available by linking to another document enabling you to judge whether the author's credentials allow him or her to speak with authority on a given topic?

Is the name of any organization given on the document you are reading? Are there headers, footers, or a distinctive watermark that show the document to be part of an official academic or scholarly Web site? Is this organization recognized in the field in which you are studying? Is this organization suitable to address the topic at hand? Can you determine the relationship between the author and the Web site? Was the document you are viewing prepared as part of the author's professional duties? Is it within his or her area of expertise?

Does this Web page actually reside in an individual's personal Internet account, rather than being part of an official website? If it's not an official website, but a personal one, this type of information resource should be approached with the greatest caution.

- **Objective reasoning**: Is the information on the site based on fact, opinion, or propaganda? It is not always easy to separate fact from opinion. Facts can usually be verified; opinions, though they may be based on factual information, evolve from the interpretation of facts. Skilled writers can make you think their interpretations are facts.
- **Research**: Does the information appear to be valid and well-researched, or is it questionable and unsupported by evidence? Assumptions should be reasonable. Note errors or omissions. Is the author's point of view objective and impartial? Is the language free of emotion-rousing words and bias?
- **Links made to other resources**: If the value of the site lies in its links to other resources, are the links kept up-to-date and made to appropriate sites? Are the links made in such a way that it is clear that an external site is being referenced? There are potential copyright issues with sites that, for instance, enclose an external link in frames so that the source of the information is unclear.
- **Reviews and awards**: What do other reviewing services say about the site? Is the site referenced and reviewed elsewhere? Has the site won any awards? If so, from which agencies? If the site has received

legitimate awards from credible organizations, the site is much more likely to be credible. Following are a few credibility evaluation sites:

Criteria to Evaluate the Credibility of WWW Resources—http://mason.gmu.edu/~montecin/web-eval-sites.htm

Guidelines for Evaluating Web Sites—http://mason.gmu.edu/~montecin/webcritique.htm

Evaluating Web Pages: Techniques to Apply & Questions to Ask—http://www.lib.berkeley.edu/TeachingLib/Guides/Internet/Evaluate.html

Step 4: *Address critical thinking skills.*

Watch a court drama or a political discussion on television and you will see critical thinking skills in action. A fact is introduced and then two sides will interpret it differently to serve their own purposes. If your students do a thorough job researching their topics, they will find many examples of conflicting interpretations of facts. This is where you can help them with their critical thinking skills.

Using our "smoking" example, here is a fact (that I am making up here for the sake of this example): "People who have smoked at least one pack of cigarettes a day for a period of 10 years or more are 40% more likely to develop lung cancer." The antismoking supporters claim this fact as proof that smoking causes lung cancer. Now the cigarette industry comes along and says, "Only 40% of smokers end up with lung cancer, but 100% of people who drank milk as babies end up with lung cancer, so if you want to get rid of lung cancer, maybe we should put warning labels on milk cartons or just outlaw milk altogether."

As students locate conflicting data interpretations, they have to develop critical thinking skills to make sense of the data they are reviewing. Following are a few strategies you can present to your students to help them make sense of the conflicting information they find:

- Distinguish between verifiable facts and interpretations of those facts.
- Distinguish relevant from irrelevant information.
- Determine the factual accuracy of a statement.
- Determine the credibility of a source.
- Identify unstated assumptions.
- Detect bias.
- Identify ambiguous claims or arguments.
- Identify logical fallacies.
- Recognize logical inconsistencies.
- Determine the strength of an argument.

Data frequently gets manipulated to produce results that support or reject an argument. Our students need to be able to identify how such information is manipulated.

Exemplary Web Sites to Promote Critical Thinking

The following links provide additional information you can use to improve your students' critical thinking skills:

Critical Thinking & Problem Solving Skills—http://falcon.jmu.edu/~ramseyil/critical.htm

Critical Thinking Skills in Education and Life—http://www.asa3.0rg/ASA/education/think/critical.htm

Practical Assessment, Research & Evaluation—http://pareonline.net/getvn.asp?v=4&n=3

Step 5: Teach organization skills.

Once students locate the information they need, they must learn how to organize and retrieve the information in a logical and manageable fashion. This includes some of the following skills:

- *Download the information to a place that is readily accessible.*
- *Store the information in a logical fashion.* Students may choose to simply create a word-processing document and store all of the information there. They can use the *Find* command to locate the part of the information they need at any time.

   They may find that a database can store their information more efficiently and make it easier to call the information up as needed. The data can be organized, sorted, and queried, making it more useful when creating a report. Spreadsheets are another alternative. They also make it easier to access information efficiently. In addition, by using charts and graphs, students can present the information visually.

- *Organize the information in presentable form.* Databases are particularly good for storing large amounts of information where it can be organized by fields.

Step 6: Teach expressive skills.

Once students locate, interpret, and store the information, they must be able to represent it as their own either in the form of media such as a computer program, video, or audio presentation or, of course, on paper in written form. Issues of copyright and academic integrity must be defined and explained to students.

One of the cornerstones of the constructivist movement in education is having students represent the knowledge they have acquired. Once a student has learned something, he should be able to present evidence of that learning in a personally relevant way to show that he really understands it in a useful way. Following are a few possibilities:

- *Write a report.* Students may simply write a report using a word processor.
- *Use presentation software.* Students may offer the information to the class verbally and supplement it with presentation software such as Microsoft PowerPoint or Apple's Keynote. Such presentation software permits students to integrate text, graphics, and video.
- *Use object-oriented authoring programs.* Programs ranging from the easy-to-use end such as HyperStudio to the professional end such as Adobe Director or Flash may be used to create interactive presentations of student findings. Using these programs, students can create multimedia projects that may include resources taken directly from the Internet.

Object-Oriented Authoring Software Links

HyperStudio—http://www.mackiev.com/hyperstudio/index.html

Adobe Director—http://www.adobe.com/products/director/

Adobe Flash—http://www.adobe.com/products/flash/

Creating Web Pages

Students may also integrate the information they have found and use it to create their own Web pages, which may be used in school intranets or posted onto a school or class Web site.

Creating WebQuests

Students may also create their own WebQuests. The following link provides a guide for creating every aspect of a WebQuest: http://webquest.org/index-create.php.

Summary

This chapter presented a problem of the mismatch between the way students like to learn and the way teachers prefer to deliver instruction. The first activity involved helping students deal with learning information that is not presented interactively and in instances where they don't control the pacing. The next two activities dealt with information delivery through the use of technology. The final activity dealt with research skills that will help make both students and teachers become lifelong learners.

As students see teachers make an effort to adapt and accommodate to them, they notice a sense of caring from those teachers. It increases their motivation. As school-related tasks more closely reflect their own, preferred ways to learn, it becomes easier for them to participate.

A Cautionary Note

Technology enthusiasts will eagerly tell you that technology can cure all of education's ills. Larry Cuban (1986) presents an engaging history of how each innovation in education was supposed to reform, rejuvenate, and revolutionize education. When we look back on the much anticipated value of radio, his point resounds. Although we believe that today's computer-based, interactive technology offers a few more advantages, here are a few things of which to be cautious.

Don't overrely on technology.

I went to a party and had a conversation with a nuclear physicist who was complaining about the newest PhDs who were working in his lab. He pointed out that when he works on a problem, he knows the answer before he even enters it into the computer, and he uses the machine to make it accurate to 12 decimal points. He says that recent graduates just accept any answer, without checking its accuracy, "Because it came from the computer." Sometimes the answers were way off and they never noticed.

The computer is a tool, not a subject.

The computer is a tool, not a topic for study. It must serve a purpose for students rather than being an end in itself. Teachers must never lose sight of the fact that we use computers as a means not an end.

The computer is not a typewriter.

The computer offers many advantages. Too many teachers think of it as an updated typewriter. Even where it replaces a typewriter for writing exercises, its real power is giving students the advantage of multiple opportunities to edit. I consider my third edit to be my first draft. Good writers know that worthwhile writing comes more from editing than initial inspiration.

References

Ames, C. (1990). Motivation: What teachers need to know. *Teachers College Record, 91*, 409–421.

Ames, C. (1992). Classrooms: Goals, structures, and student motivation. *Journal of Educational Psychology, 84*, 261–271.

Anderson, J. R. (2005). *Cognitive psychology and its implications* (6th ed.). New York: Worth.

Ausebel, D. (1968). *Educational psychology: A cognitive view.* New York: Holt, Rinehart & Winston.

Bandura, A. (1977). Self-efficacy: Toward a unifying theory of behavioral change. *Psychological Review, 84*, 191–215.

Bandura, A. (1997). *Self-efficacy: The exercise of control.* New York: Freeman.

Bruning, R. H., Schraw, G. J., Norby, M. M., & Ronning, R. R. (2004). *Cognitive psychology and instruction* (4th ed.). Upper Saddle River, NJ: Merrill/Prentice Hall.

Cassady, J. (1999). *The effects of examples as elaboration in text on memory and learning.* Paper presented at the annual meeting of the American Educational Research Association, Montreal, Canada.

Cochrane, T. (2005). *Podcasting: Do it yourself guide.* New York: Wiley.

Cooper, H. M., & Tom, D. Y. H. (1984). Teacher expectation research: A review with implications for classroom instruction. *The Elementary School Journal, 85*(1), 76–89.

Cooper, J., Robinson, P., & Ball, D. (2003). *Small group instruction in higher education.* Stillwater, OK: New Forums Press.

Cuban, L. (1986). *Teachers and machines: The classroom use of technology since 1920.* New York: Teachers College Press.

Davidson, J., & Sternberg, R. (2003). *The psychology of problem solving.* Cambridge, England: Cambridge University Press.

Deci, E., & Ryan, R. (1985). *Intrinsic motivation and self-determination in human behavior.* New York: Plenum Press.

Deci, E., & Ryan, R. (1991). A motivational approach to self: Integration in personality. In R. Dienstbier (Ed.), *Nebraska Symposium on Motivation 1990* (Vol. 38, pp. 237–288). Lincoln: University of Nebraska Press.

Deci, E., & Ryan, R. (Eds.). (2002). *Handbook of self-determination research.* Rochester, NY: University of Rochester Press.

Dembo, M. H., & Eaton, M. J. (2000). Self-regulation of academic learning in middle-level schools. *The Elementary School Journal, 100*(3), 473–490.

Desberg, P., Colbert, J., & Trimble, K. (1995). *Interactive case studies: Classroom Management.* Boston: Allyn & Bacon.

Desberg, P., & Fisher, F. (2001). *Teaching with technology: A web-based resource for teachers* (3rd ed.). Boston: Allyn & Bacon.

Desberg, P., & Taylor, J. H. (1986). *Essentials of task analysis.* Lanham, MD: University Press of America.

Dodge, B. (2007). Interview in *Education World.* Retrieved February 2, 2009, from http://www.educationworld.com/a_issues/chat/chat015.shtml

Driscoll, M. (2005). *Psychology of learning for instruction* (3rd ed.). Boston: Allyn & Bacon.

Eccles, J., & Wigfield, A. (2001). Motivational beliefs, values, and goals. *Annual Review of Psychology, 53,* 109–132.

Emmer, E. T., & Gerwels, M. C. (2002). Cooperative learning in elementary classrooms: Teaching practices and lesson characteristics. *The Elementary School Journal, 103*(1), 75–92.

Emmer, E. T., & Stough, L. M. (2001). Classroom management: A critical part of educational psychology with implications for teacher education. *Educational Psychologist, 36,* 103–112.

Festinger, L. (1957). *A theory of cognitive dissonance.* Palo Alto, CA: Stanford University Press.

Fogg, B. J. (2002). *Persuasive technology: Using computers to change what we think and do.* San Francisco: Morgan Kaufman.

Ford, M. E. (1995). Advances in motivation theory and research: Implications for special education professionals. *Intervention in School and Clinic, 31,* 70–83.

Freud, S. (1966). *The complete introductory lectures on psychoanalysis.* New York: Norton.

Gladwell, M. (2005). *Blink: The power of thinking without thinking.* New York: Back Bay Books.

Good, T., & Brophy, J. (2003). Looking in classrooms (9th ed.) Boston: Allyn & Bacon.

Hull, C. (1951). *Essentials of behavior.* New Haven. CT: Yale University Press.

Hull, C. (1952). *A behavioral system: An introduction to behavior theory concerning the individual organism.* New Haven, CT: Yale University Press.

Johnson, S. (2006). *Everything bad is good for you: How today's popular culture is actually making us smarter.* New York: Riverhead.

Johnston, S. (2003). A crisis of clarity. In J. Cooper (Ed.), Higher education: Lessons from the past, visions of the future (pp. 349–366). Stillwater, OK: New Forums Press.

Johnston, S., & Cooper, J. (1997). Quick-Thinks: Active thinking in lecture classes and televised instruction. *Cooperative Learning and College Teaching, 8*(1), 2–6.

Karau, S. J., & Williams, K. D. (1993). Social loafing: A meta-analytic review and theoretical integration. *Journal of Personality and Social Psychology, 65*(4), 681–706.

Keyser, V., & Barling, J. (1981). Determinants of children's self-efficacy beliefs in an academic environment. *Cognitive Therapy and Research, 5,* 29–40.

Kuklinski, M. R., & Weinstein, R. S. (2001). Classroom and developmental differences in a path model of teacher expectancy effects. *Child Development, 72*(5), 1554–1578.

Leary, M. R. (1996). *Self-presentation: Impression management and interpersonal behavior.* Boulder, CO: Westview Press.

Leu, D. (2005). *New literacies, reading research, and the challenges of change: A deictic perspective.* Retrieved February 9, 2009, from http://www.newliteracies .uconn.edu/events.html

Leu, D. J., Kinzer, C. K., Coiro, J. L., & Cammack, D. W. (2004). Toward a theory of new literacies emerging from the internet and other information and communication technologies. In N. J. Unrau & R. B. Ruddell (Eds.), *Theoretical models and processes of reading* (5th ed., 1568–1611). Newark, DE: International Reading Association.

Lovaas, I. (2002). *Teaching individuals with developmental delays: Basic intervention techniques.* Dallas, TX: Pro-Ed.

MacGregor, J., Cooper, J., Smith, K., & Robinson, P. (2000). *Strategies for energizing large classes.* San Francisco: Jossey-Bass.

Mach, N., Desberg, P., Cantor, J., Davis, J., Hembacher, D., & Moscovici, H. (2005, October). *Preparing teachers to integrate technology into multicultural inner-city classrooms.* Paper presented at the Conference of Urban and Metropolitan Universities, Los Angeles.

McClelland, D., Koestner, R., & Weinberger, J. (1989). How do self-attributed and implicit motives differ? *Psychological Review, 96,* 69–702.

McKenzie, J. (1999). *Beyond technology: Questioning, research, and the information literate school.* Bellingham, WA: FNO Press.

Mowrer, O. H. (1960). *Learning theory and behavior.* New York: Wiley.

O'Reilly, T., Symons, S., & MacLatchy-Gaudet, H. (1998). A comparison of self-explanation and elaborative interrogation. *Contemporary Educational Psychology, 23,* 443–445.

Palincsar, A. (1998). Social constructivist perspectives on teaching and learning. *Annual Review of Psychology, 49,* 345–375.

Pintrich, P. R. (1989). The dynamic interplay of student motivation and cognition in the college classroom. In C. Ames & M. L. Maehr (Eds.), *Advances in motivation and achievement: Motivation enhancing environments* (Vol. 6, pp. 117–160). Greenwich, CT: JAI Press.

Pintrich, P. R. (1999). The role of motivation in promoting and sustaining self-regulated learning. *International Journal of Educational Research, 31,* 459–470.

Pintrich, P. R., & Schunk, D. H. (2002). *Motivation in education: Theory, research, and applications* (2nd ed.). Upper Saddle River, NJ: Merrill/Prentice Hall.

Rogers, C. R. (1963). The actualizing tendency in relation to "motives" and to consciousness. In M. R. Jones (Ed.), *Nebraska Symposium on Motivation* (Vol. 11, pp. 1–24). Lincoln: University of Nebraska Press.

Rogoff, B. (1998). Cognition as a collaborative process. In D. Kuhn & R. S. Sieglar (Eds.), *Handbook of child psychology* (5th ed., Vol. 2, pp. 679–744). New York: Wiley.

Ryan, A. M. (2001). The peer group as a context for the development of young adolescent motivation and achievement. *Child Development, 72,* 1135–1150.

Ryan, R., & Deci, E. (2000). Intrinsic and extrinsic motivation: Classic definitions and new directions. *Contemporary Educational Psychology, 25,* 54–67.

Schachter, S. (1964). The interaction of cognitive and physiological determinants of emotional state. In L. Berkowitz (Ed.), *Advances in experimental social psychology* (Vol. 1, pp. 49–80). New York: Academic Press.

Schneider, W., & Bjorklund, D. F. (2003). Memory and knowledge development. In J. Valsiner & K. Connolly (Eds.), *Handbook of developmental psychology* (pp. 370–403). London: Sage.

Shulman, L. S. (1995). Just in case: Reflections on learning from experience. In J. Colbert, P. Desberg, & K. Trimble (Eds.), *The case for education: Contemporary approaches for using case methods* (pp. 197–217). Boston: Allyn & Bacon.

Stipek, D. (2002). *Motivation to learn* (4th ed.). Boston: Allyn & Bacon.

Terry, S. (2006). *Learning and memory: Basic principles, processes and procedures* (3rd ed.). Boston: Allyn & Bacon.

Thorndike, E. L. (1913). *Educational psychology: Vol. 2. The psychology of learning.* New York: Teachers College Press.

Tollefson, N. (2000). Classroom applications of cognitive theories of motivation. *Educational Psychology Review, 12,* 63–83.

Tolman, E. C. (1932). *Purposive behavior in animals and men.* New York: Appleton-Century-Crofts (Reprinted 1949, 1951, University of California Press, Berkeley).

Vygotsky, L. S. (1962). *Thought and language.* Cambridge, MA: MIT Press.

Weiner, B. (1979). A theory of motivation for some classroom experiences. *Journal of Educational Psychology, 71,* 3–25.

Weiner, B. (1986). *An attributional theory of motivation and emotion.* New York: Springer-Verlag.

Weiner, B. (2000). Interpersonal and intrapersonal theories of motivation from an attributional perspective. *Educational Psychology Review, 12,* 1–14.

Weiner, B., & Graham, S. (1989). Understanding the motivational role of affect: Life-Span research from an attributional perspective. *Cognition and Emotion, 3*(4), 401–419.

Wigfield, A., & Eccles, J. (1992). The development of achievement task values: A theoretical analysis. *Developmental Review, 12,* 265–310.

Wigfield, A., & Eccles, J. (2000). Expectancy-value theory of achievement motivation. *Contemporary Educational Psychology, 25,* 68–81.

Wood, D., Bruner, J., & Ross, S. (1976). The role of tutoring in problem solving. *British Journal of Psychology, 66,* 181–196.

Woolfolk, A. (2008). *Educational psychology: Active learning edition.* Boston: Allyn & Bacon.

Zimmerman, B. J. (1990). Self-regulated learning and academic achievement: An overview. *Educational Psychologist, 25,* 3–17.